OUT OF THE

HOWLING STORM

POEMS BY

Bei Dao, Yang Lian, Shu Ting,

Jiang He, Gu Cheng, Duo Duo,

Mang Ke, Chou Ping, Xi Chuan,

Zhang Zhen, Tang Yaping,

Fei Ye, Bei Ling, and Ha Jin

EDITED BY

TONY BARNSTONE

Wesleyan University Press

Published by University Press of New England

Hanover and London

Out of the Howling Storm

The New Chinese Poetry

Wesleyan University Press
Published by University Press of New England, Hanover, NH 03755
© 1993 by Wesleyan University
All rights reserved
Printed in the United States of America 5 4 3 2 1
CIP data appear at the end of the book

For

WILLIS   BARNSTONE

and

SARAH   HANDLER,

best friends and

companions in China

CONTENTS

THE MISTY POETS

Bei Dao

(translated by Bonnie McDougall and Chen Maiping, with exceptions noted)

Yang Lian

(translated by Tony Barnstone and Newton Liu)

Shu Ting

(translated by Tony Barnstone and Newton Liu, with exceptions noted)

Jiang He

Gu Cheng

Duo Duo

Mang Ke

THE POST-MISTY POETS

Chou Ping

Xi Chuan

(translated by Tony Barnstone and the author, with exception noted)

Zhang Zhen

(translated by Tony Barnstone and Newton Liu)

Tang Yaping

(translated by Tony Barnstone and Newton Liu)

Fei Ye

Bei Ling

Ha Jin

ACKNOWLEDGMENTS

I WOULD LIKE to thank Willis Barnstone for his incisive suggestions on the introduction and translations, James A. Wilson for his support and friendship from the inception of this project and for giving this collection its title, Newton Liu, my primary co-translator, for his good humor and good advice on the book, Sandy Seaton for his friendship and help in publishing a number of these translations, and C. H. Kwock and Aliki Barnstone for moral support. To Ayame Fukuda for supporting me in every way possible, as proofreader, sounding board, adviser, and friend, I owe a debt larger than I can express. I'd like as well to thank Michelle Yeh, one of the few scholars in the English speaking world who is giving these poets the critical attention they deserve, for her encouragement and for an enlightening correspondence. Finally, I would like to extend special thanks to Donald Finkel, for his extraordinarily generous support for this project, for his unconditional friendship, and for doing his best to help out when things had bogged down in a permissions nightmare.

The introduction appeared in an earlier form in *The Centennial Review* (Vol. 36, No. 1, Winter 1992), and some parts of it appeared in *Nimrod* (Vol. 29, No. 2, Spring/Summer 1986) in an article entitled "Everyone is Writing." A version of "Translation as Forgery" appeared in *Poetry Flash* (No. 239, February 1993). Some of these poems have appeared before, sometimes in earlier versions, in the following literary journals: *American Poetry Review*: Mang Ke, "Darling," "To Children," "Yesterday and Today"; *Beloit Poetry Review*: Duo Duo, "When People Rise from Cheese, Statement #1"; *The Literary Review*: Chou Ping, "Ways of Looking at a Poet," Tang Yaping, "Black Night," "Black Swamp," "Black Nightgown," "Black Cave," Zhang Zhen, "A Desire," "The New," "Abortion"; *Nimrod*: Shu Ting, "Dream of an Island," Bei Ling, "I Don't Need This"; *Representations*: Mang Ke, "Ape Herd," Gu Cheng, "Who'd Have Thought?," "Discovery," "Bulin Met Bandit," "Bulin Is Dead, It Seems"; *AGNI*: Ha Jin, "Marching Toward Martyrdom."

The editor gratefully acknowledges the following presses for rights to reprint works. Reprinted by permission of the University of Chicago Press: from Ha Jin, *Between Silences*, copyright © 1990 by Ha Jin. Reprinted by permission of New Directions Publishing Corporation and David Higham Associates (international rights): from Bei Dao, *Old Snow: Poems by Bei Dao*, translated by Bonnie S. McDougall and Chen Maiping, copyright © 1991 by Bei Dao. Reprinted by permission of New Directions Publishing Corporation and Anvil Press (international rights): from Bei Dao, *The August Sleepwalker: Poems by Bei Dao*, translated by Bonnie S. McDougall, copyright © 1988 by Bei Dao. "The Oranges Are Ripe" and "Answer" by Bei Dao, reprinted by permission of North Point Press, a division of Farrar, Straus & Giroux, Inc.: from *A Splintered Mirror*, translated by Donald Finkel, copyright © 1991 by Donald Finkel. Reprinted by permission of Renditions Paperbacks: from *Selected Poems* by Gu Cheng, edited by Sean Golden and Chu Chiyu, copyright © 1990 by the Chinese University of Hong Kong. Reprinted by permission of University of Washington Press: from Julia Lin, *Modern Chinese Poetry: An Introduction*, copyright © 1972. "Beyond" and "Midnight Singer" reprinted by permission of Harold Ober Associates and David Higham Associates (international rights), copyright 1993 by Bei Dao, translation copyright 1993 by Donald Finkel and Xueliang Chen.

TRANSLATION AS FORGERY

Comments from the Editor

IN "The Work of Art in the Age of Mechanical Reproduction," Walter Benjamin laments the loss of the original work of art's "aura" as it passes through the machine and comes out the other end multiplied. When "The cathedral leaves its locale to be received in the studio of a lover of art" it is somehow diminished by this act of photographic reproduction. Life becomes *Life* magazine. The live performance of musicians, playing off the energy and emotions of their audience, becomes a mass-reproduced "live album" in which the audience is only ficticiously present, as in the canned laugh track on a television sitcom.

Some tendentious aspects of Benjamin's argument may seem dated today (are the movies really fascist in nature?), but at the heart of the essay is a questioning of where we find *value* in art, a question that remains of particular interest in postmodern culture, and pertinent to the act of translation itself. Is it possible, as Benjamin says, that the very nature of reality is warped and diminished by the act of reproduction, that somehow reality itself becomes a forgery? I think of a scene I saw some years back in a movie by Santa Cruz video artist Chip Lord, in which he is cruising into Los Angeles and meditating on the serene California landscapes he is driving through. All these locations, with the value that they derive simply by being where they are, have been fodder for generations of location scouts who turn them into movie sets, until in driving past them you catch ghost images of countless movies, seeing not reality but, as Chip Lord says, "image after image after image," until all that is left of reality is an afterimage. Is translation necessarily just such an afterimage?

"[W]hat is really jeopardized" by reproduction, according to Benjamin, "is the authority of the object." Art's esthetic value is of course not equal to its monetary value, but, like gold or diamonds, it derives much of its value from its uniqueness. Dollars physically represent to us the abstract concept of value, and, until the decline of bimetallism in the United States, this value was guaranteed by the citizen's right to freely exchange them for their equivalent in gold. What Fort Knox filled with genius can guarantee the reader that the translation is a fair exchange for gold? Alexander the Great first came up with the practice of stamping his face on coins of the realm. Money has power so long as the face on the coin guarantees the coin is good. But what guarantees that it can be freely exchanged for coin of another realm? Later, Roman emperors took to defacing statuary depicting the faces of their predecessors, replacing the old heads with their own likenesses. The translator's task is the opposite; we efface our presence as assiduously as master forgers trying not to get caught.

Since the erosion of the gold standard in the United States, the value of currency is much more closely linked to the size of the sum total of all printed currency. If you print too much currency, you get inflation. Similarly, master printmakers make a point of defacing or destroying their templates after making a limited edition so as to maintain, if not a uniqueness, at least a limited hemorrhaging of the works' value through reproduction. The signature at the bottom of the work, like that of the Treasurer and the Secretary of the Treasury on the dollar bill, indicates that it is an *author*ized reproduction, not a forgery. I might offer to trade you a photocopy of a hundred dollar bill for your real one—after all, they look the same—but, chances are, you'd turn me down.

In literature there is no original to be reproduced, there is only the text, which is designed to be a reproduction—as if no handpainted Mona Lisa were on display in the Louvre and Da Vinci's masterpiece existed only in cheap postcard reproductions for sale in the museum shop. The "Uniqueness and permanance" that Benjamin celebrates don't lie in ink on the page; the very nature of "text" is that "transitoriness and reproducibility" that he abhors. Certainly if I owned one of the hand-printed and hand-inked editions of Blake's *Songs of Innocence and of Experience* I would have in my hands a valuable object of art, and chances are that the experience of reading it would seem more valuable than the experience of reading a copy of the admirable Trianon Press color reproduction, but this is itself an anomaly, based on the momentary marriage of art and literature. The text itself is transcendental, briefly inhabiting editions of the work. It may suffer typesetter errors and editorial changes, yet these do not essentially change the work of genius, because that genius lies in the organs, the nervous system, the neural net of *language* itself, not in the particular tattoos marking a particular book's paper skin. Thus, in translation, in spite of the fact that the original has no physical presence, one must worry again about "authority," about the signature of the author's style and vision that may be fatally lost in the transformation from language to language. Even though literary texts have no physical original, translation, that long-despised activity, is as much a forgery as the dollar bill you run off on the printing press in your basement. The question then becomes how to make an *inspired* forgery, like artist J. S. G. Boggs, who draws his own hundred dollar bills with colored ink and pencils, runs off limited editions on color photocopy machines and then has remarkable success in spending his forgeries, by convincing waiters, shop owners, even his landlord, to exchange their services for his currency at the written "value."

In literature, somehow, we have always been in a postmodern world in which the central value exchange is not my fur for your pound of meat, or even my fur for your paper money, but always paper for paper, words for words, abstraction for abstraction. The world, abstracted into language, is written into a poem which you read and abstract to fit your own experience. In translation in particular the exchange of one abstract value for another is central to the process—is the process itself. Yet in this process, something is considered to be lost—the way with each successive generation of cassette tape reproduction the ratio of "hiss" to original sound goes up. Unlike the work in translation, the work of art in the original language is thought of as unique and permanent. Thus the great works of literature must be translated again for every generation, for those who cannot read them in the original.

In translation the achievement of the author is already filtered through another language and, what is worse, another mind. In spite of literature's transcendental nature, we come back to Benjamin's aura, to the loss of "presence." I have found this to be a particular issue in editing and translating these poems, many of them political in nature. How to bring them to the other side intact, these little worlds urged into being by specific campaigns, such as Mao's Cultural Revolution campaign against romance in literature and the mass media, or by pervasive propaganda metaphors that have no meaning in the United States, such as the once widespread comparison of the masses to fields of sunflowers whose heads follow the sun (Mao Zedong) across the sky? Ideally the poem should be "present" to us even if the esthetic, political, and cultural contexts out of which it grew are absent, but sometimes this just isn't so. In these cases I do my best to provide such contexts with limited notes and a long introduction. I don't like attaching notes to poems; I believe that even in translation a poem should stand on its own as an esthetic entity, but sometimes it can't be helped. The note is to the poem as the voice of the pundit is to the raw images of students at Tiananmen Square.

Even the political events at Tiananmen Square, many of them filmed "live," could not have had such global impact if such an act of translation had not occurred. The 1989 Democracy Movement in China was the first armchair revolution, in which millions watched worldwide as the unarmed students faced off against tanks and soldiers, armed only with idealism and hope, giving the lie to the popular song's refrain, "The revolution will not be televised." Certainly the students would have been crushed long before they were had it not been for the presence of this international audience, and for the fact that these great events were captured on video camera, converted into digital codes, and transmitted to your home, where they were reinterpreted by the pixels of your television screen. The poems you read in this book have traveled from Tiananmen Square to your living room through a similar act of translation, and necessarily they have changed into another life in their journey into the underworld of language and back. They are changed even by my attaching these comments to them, as, when "things fall apart," the nature and velocity of history's gyre is determined by the spin doctors and talking heads. And yet, as in the case of the video cameras at Tiananmen, I think some value lies in the activity.

The thing to remember is that some forgeries are works of art. After all, Gabriel Garcia Marquez has said of Gregory Rabassa's English translation of *One Hundred Years of Solitude* that it reads better than the original Spanish! I cannot give you the poem itself any more than I can give you the Mona Lisa. But what I have strived to do throughout in making difficult choices among alternate translations is to find a middle ground between those which are word for word cribs of the original but in which the reproduced words lose their aura, and those which attempt to write a poem in English but in which that subjective entity, the author's presence, is "lost in the translation." The author may be dead, as Foucault has said, but as I see it there is no reason to trample on the corpse.

Yet there is always the hope for the translator that, through concentration and dedication, she or he might come to the point where the dead author guides the pen across the page like an invisible spirit moving the pointer on a Ouija board. The "aura," finally, is what makes the poem live, though nations and revolutions die out. Will the spirit that moved millions in Tiananmen Square and across China speak again? I can't say, though I hope. Does the author's spirit speak to and through you in the poems collected here? In this question you have the final authority.   T.B.

BIOGRAPHICAL NOTES

BEI DAO is the pen name of Zhao Zhenkai. He was born in 1949 in Beijing, and was a construction worker for some years during the Cultural Revolution. During the Peking Spring of 1979 he started the famous underground literary magazine *Jintian* (Today) and soon became the leading poet of the 1980s. With the new acceptance of Chinese Modernism and the thaw in official censorship that came in the middle 1980s, he gained mainstream acceptance, editing an official magazine and becoming a member of the Chinese Writers' Association. During the summer 1989 Democracy Movement he was overseas at a writer's conference and has elected to remain in exile from China. His work has been widely translated and anthologized, and two collections of his poetry, *The August Sleep-walker* (1988) and *Old Snow* (1991), are available from New Directions. His fiction has also appeared with New Directions. He has just left Norway to live in Denmark. A new collection of his poems, translated by Donald Finkel, is forthcoming from New Directions.

YANG LIAN, one of the original Misty poets, is currently living in New Zealand, teaching at the University of Auckland. Born in Beijing, he was sent down to the countryside during the Cultural Revolution, where he began to write poetry. His two books are *The Ritual Spirit* and *The Spirit in the Wilderness*.

SHU TING is the pen name of Gong Peiyu, who was born in 1952. She was the leading woman poet in China in the 1980s. A southeast Fujian native, she was sent to the countryside during the Cultural Revolution before she graduated from junior high school. Then she worked in a cement factory and later a textile mill. In 1979 she published her first poem and in 1983 was asked to be a professional writer by the Writers' Association,

Fujian Branch, of which she now is the deputy chairperson. Her collections of poetry include *Brigantines* (1982) and *Selected Lyrics of Shu Ting and Gu Cheng* (1985). She won the National Poetry Award in 1981 and 1983.

JIANG HE is the pen name of Yu Youze, who was born in 1949 in Beijing. A high school graduate, he was a factory worker for some years. He is one of the most influential young poets of the 1980s, often mentioned along with Bei Dao, Shu Ting, Gu Cheng, and Yang Lian as one of the five leading poets of the time. He currently lives in New York City.

GU CHENG, son of the army veteran poet Gu Gong, was born in 1956 in Beijing. After elementary school, he went to the coast country in Shandong where he started writing poetry at a very early age. In a self-imposed exile after the Tiananmen Square massacre, he now lives in New Zealand. He has had poems published in many magazines and anthologies. He is co-author of *Selected Lyrics by Shu Ting and Gu Cheng* (1985) and of *Selected Poems of Bei Dao and Gu Cheng* (Switzerland, 1981); a collection of his selected poems has appeared in English, published by Renditions Paperbacks of the Chinese University of Hong Kong (1990).

DUO DUO is the pen name of Li Shizheng. He was born in Beijing in 1951. At the outbreak of the Cultural Revolution he was separated from his parents and sent to the countryside. He returned to Beijing in 1971, where he worked on short stories, poetry, and screenplays, and for some time was a reporter for *The Peasant Daily*. *Looking Out from Death: From the Cultural Revolution to Tiananmen Square*, a collection of his poems in English translation, appeared with Bloomsbury Press in 1989. He is currently living in Holland, teaching at the University of Leiden.

MANG KE is the pen name of Jiang Shiwei. He was born in 1951 and is one of the best known younger poets of China. With Bei Dao he was co-editor of *Jintian* (Today), an underground literary journal that appeared in the "Beijing Spring" of 1979 and that the government closed down in 1980. He spent the Cultural Revolution, like so many others, in internal exile in the countryside, and then returned to Beijing. Unlike Bei Dao, his work was never officially recognized and has appeared in China substantially in underground mimeographed copies, or *samizdat*, to borrow a Russian term, though some poems have appeared in official magazines. His poems in translation have appeared in *American Poetry Review*, *Representations*, and *Nimrod*.

CHOU PING was born in Changsha City, Hunan Province, in 1957. He writes poetry both in Chinese and in English, and his poetry and translations of Chinese poetry into English have appeared in such American journals as the *Literary Review* and *Nimrod*. In 1983 he studied English language and literature in the Advanced Teachers' Training Program at Beijing Foreign Language University, where he studied poetry with Willis Barnstone. After that he taught at Xiangtang Teachers' College, Hunan Province, until fall 1991, when he enrolled in the Ph.D. program in English at Indiana University in Bloomington, Indiana.

XI CHUAN is a poet, translator, and a graduate of the English Literature program at Beijing University. His book of poems, *The Chinese Rose*, was published in 1991. He is working as an editor for *Globe Magazine* of the Xinhua News Agency. His poetry and his translations of Chinese poetry into English have appeared in *Nimrod* as well as a number of Chinese journals and anthologies. He was awarded the October Prize for literature by the *October Bimonthly*, one of the top Chinese literary magazines. In 1988 with some friends he started an unofficial poetry magazine named *Tendency*, which the Security Bureau closed down in 1992. Now he is co-editing another unofficial nationwide poetry magazine called *Modern Han Poetry*. His translations of the poetry of Ezra Pound and of Jorge Luis Borges have been published in Chinese magazines.

ZHANG ZHEN is a Shanghai native. After studying journalism at Fudan University, where she was involved with the Poetry Society, she emigrated to Sweden with her husband in 1983 and studied languages and filmmaking there. From 1985 to 1988, returning to China, she lived and worked in Beijing (at a foreign news bureau), where she was active in the literary and artistic scene. In the following three years she lived and studied in Japan, and is currently a graduate student in Comparative Literature at the University of Iowa. She started writing poetry in 1980, and more recently has translated poems from Swedish and English into Chinese. She is a regular contributor to *Jintian* (Today), the newly revived (and now foreign-based) Chinese language literary journal that was so important in the Beijing Spring of 1979 and that serves now as a prime forum for overseas Chinese writers.

TANG YAPING, born in 1962 in Sichuan, graduated from Sichuan University as a philosophy major in 1983. She is currently working as an editor at the Guizhou television station in the Southwest of China.

FEI YE, translator of Osip Mandelstam and other Russian poets into Chinese, comes from Heilungjian Province in Northeastern China. After trouble with the Chinese authorities he emigrated to Berkeley, California, to live with his wife, and founded the organization Chinese Writers in Exile. He is currently serving a five-year sentence in California for assault.

BEI LING, or Huang Bei Ling, is a graduate of Beijing University. He is one of the younger generation who took their esthetic cue from the Misty (*menglong*) school of poets. He recently emigrated to the United States, where he is currently poet-in-residence at Brown University. During the Beijing Spring of 1979 he was involved in the Democracy movement as a reporter for *Spring of Beijing*, an underground political magazine, and as an editor of *China Human Rights*, an underground magazine. He has edited two collections of contemporary Chinese poetry, published underground in 1984 and 1985, and is currently working on a personal memoir (titled *Underground*) of the activities of the Chinese intellectuals and artists who participated in the Democracy Wall movement in China. His work was first published in underground literary journals in China in 1979, especially in *Jintian* (Today), and a number of his poems in translation have appeared in *Nimrod* and in *New Tide: Contemporary Chinese Poetry*, a Canadian publication. His poetry collection *Today and Tomorrow* was published in China in 1988.

HA JIN was born in 1956 in Liaoning. The son of an army officer, he entered the People's Army early in the Cultural Revolution at a time when the schools were closed, worked as a telegraph operator for some time, then went back to school, earning a B.A. and an M.A. He is currently a Ph.D. candidate at Brandeis University in English and American literature. His book of poems, *Between Silences: A Voice from China*, appeared with the University of Chicago Press in 1990. He has also won a Pushcart Prize for his fiction.

OUT OF THE

HOWLING STORM

INTRODUCTION

Chinese Poetry Through the Looking Glass

IT WAS AT LEAST in part the ironic prospect of spending 1984, Orwell's year, in Beijing that first sent me over the ocean, jobless, near penniless, flying on hope. Fresh out of college, I wanted to go very far away, leaving everything familiar behind, and was banking on a hunch that through a combination of bluff and imagination I would be able to land a job in journalism or in teaching to support me through the year. I was lucky. Though China was in the midst of ever-expanding relations with the United States there was a dearth of qualified teachers of English. I found myself teaching language and literature at one of Beijing's best schools, the Beijing Foreign Studies University, where future diplomats and professional interpreters were groomed. Within a few weeks I was the proud owner of a green Flying Pigeon bicycle, pedaling to work down Beijing's wide, poplar-lined boulevards, side by side with thousands upon thousands of bicycle-mounted commuters.

I didn't know quite what to expect of this country, China, where one fourth of the world's people lived. Western visions of China have been consistently distorted by the lens of Western politics and interest; and I found it hard at times to trust the reports of a Western press that had been recording China's shift toward capitalism with much gleeful editorializing and little objective reporting, and of course the Chinese press (as generations of China-watchers can attest) is notoriously full of disinformation, and is useful mainly as an indicator of current government policy. To get anything out of the Chinese press, you must engage in a kind of negative reading: you assume you are reading lies and yet, by analyzing how the article is trying to manipulate its target audience, you sometimes can intuit the true events that lie behind it. I didn't expect to find the Orwellian case of social engineering gone madly wrong that the cold war pundits described, and I knew I wouldn't find the socialist utopia that American radicals in the

'60s, sporting Mao caps and little red books of "Mao Zedong thought," envisioned there. These extremist views have more to say about the stereotyping of cultural difference than about China per se. Dystopia or utopia, Fu Manchu or Charlie Chan, the meaning of China for the West has been more a litmus test of Western concerns than of Chinese realities. In Enlightenment Europe, faraway China, about which very little was actually known, was depicted by Goldsmith, Leibnitz, Voltaire, and others as a kind of Ur-empire of Enlightenment ideals ruled over by cultured and rational benevolent Emperors, an example to the West of a society whose moral structure was based on reason, not religion.[1] Coleridge's Xanadu (actually the royal summer palace at Chengde) depicted China in the comfortable Romantic model of the exotic East, redolent of opium and decadence. This exoticism, deriving from medieval travelers' tales, has proved to be the most durable myth of China. It is manifested in the alien figure of Sax Rohmer's Fu Manchu, the effeminate, exotic mastermind with his plots to unite the East against the colonial West. A more benevolent version of it appears in the innumerable poems by Western poets in which what is sexual, sublime, or merely different takes the name of China. Thus, Richard Wilbur for example, in "Digging for China," makes China all that is not New Jersey, and tries to dig a hole there in his back yard, until, exhausted, reeling with vertigo, he sees his yard magically transformed into a world he had never seen. Though still in his back yard in New Jersey, "all [he] could see was China, China, China."

Let it be said at the outset, then, that this window onto China must be defined less by what it opens onto than by what its frame excludes. In introducing the new Chinese poets here, I have chosen to highlight political aspects of their poetry and of their esthetic stances, although they write many poems that are not political in nature. Yet, as we will see, due to China's troubled literary history, the use of a common metaphor in unsanctioned ways, a poet's experimentation with Modernist techniques eschewed by the official literary establishment, even the writing of a simple love poem can be a dangerous political act. In focusing this discussion on China's troubled history of censorship and repression in the arts I give a limited version of China, yet it is essential to an understanding of themes of social apocalypse and redemption that so often appear in the new Chinese poetry, and of why this poetry is so innovative and important. Having translated the poems on and off for the past eight years, I find it also necessary to translate the context out of which the poems grew. Many of these poems are ephemeral, glancing encounters with brutality, an execution in half-light, a nightmare glimpsed through the mists; thus their authors have been nicknamed the "Misty" poets.[2] As we part the mists to see what they hide, we should be aware of how this obscures other aspects of that problematic entity, "China."

The China I found was one that partook of all its myths and surpassed them all, a society in the midst of great change. Some aspects of the Revolution had backfired, so that a society in which money brought power had given way to one in which connections and access constituted power. Though an army general might make nearly the same salary as a janitor, and might actually *own* very little, he had *access* to limousines, palatial subsidized housing, Western movies, and secret supermarkets stocked with only the choicest foods. Although on the surface China had become a classless, egalitarian society, the old feudal class privileges had been transferred to a new nobility, in which privilege equaled coming from the family of a revolutionary hero or a high Party member, and in which the relatives of landlords and the old nobility had become the new class of untouchables. For the rest, access to good medical care, special foods, theatre tickets, or good jobs was predicated on what connections (*guanxi*) they had. Side by side with the surface economy was a pervasive underground economy, the "back door," a black market system of exchange of favors and material bribes made necessary by the fact that the front door was kept locked against the ordinary person. An echo of feudal class structure was still heard from the clicking of five-inch fingernails on bureaucrats' desk-tops— signs that they were not of that low class that worked with their hands— and though this was a "People's Republic," policed by a "People's Army," the people found themselves politically disenfranchised, without recourse due to the lack of a functioning democracy or legal system to make the government accountable for its actions.

Yet China had taken a new economic path with the rise to power of Deng Xiaoping, and, as the old verities of socialism were dismantled in favor of a society embracing limited capitalism, there was the sense that anything and everything could be, and was being, changed. 1984 didn't live up to Orwellian predictions. Although 1983 saw the repressive "Anti-Spiritual Pollution Campaign" in which experimental and Western-influenced writers, artists, and filmmakers were severely criticized, 1984 and early 1985 proved to be a time of remarkable opening up. Signs of it were everywhere. From my perspective as a teacher I noticed most how the literature syllabi had changed from a preponderance of texts that could be interpreted as critical of Western economics and liberalism—Zola, Dreiser, Dickens—to key texts of individualism—Thoreau, Emerson, Whitman. And, though this may seem to be a small thing, fashion, that sure sign of ideology, was changing as well—from white shirts under the uniform blue or gray of Mao jackets to diverse colorful garments, even Mickey Mouse teeshirts from Hong Kong. Even more striking as an exterior sign of the nascent search for individual difference was the way that as the semester progressed my students started appearing in class, one after another, with rather badly permed hair, although in the past, noted a *China Daily* article about the new trend, "permanent waves and other beauty services were . . . regarded as degenerate."[3] Authorities even tolerated a rock-and-roll band called the Beijing Underground, a remarkable thing for a society that had been so closed to the outside world that the last Western dance and music craze to penetrate it had been the tango. I should note, though, that at one concert police arrested several young people for dancing, and forced the band to change its name in the end, under the mistaken assumption that it referred to the secret system of underground tunnels built under Beijing in case of nuclear attack. Friends and students for the most part felt comfortable speaking to me, candidly, in private and in class, though one of my best students who had ceased to attend class took me aside in private one day to tell me not to think badly about her, but that she had to drop the class because she had been denounced to the Party by some unnamed informant for speaking too freely in discussion section. In spite of these mixed signals, for a brief and ultimately illusory period it seemed as if the process of conversion to the economics of liberalism might jumble things up enough that the liberal freedoms might slip through the cracks as well.

For several years prior to my arrival the literary journals had been filled with debates about the new movement of literary Modernism in China, as the old entrenched Social Realists attacked the obscurities of the "Misty" (*meng long*) poets, and as critics took part in a general attack on the ideological invasion of European and American Modernism in translation, which younger poets, novelists, even journalists, had begun to imitate and transform. Here one old school critic bewails the new writing's embracing of the subjective:

they . . . emphasiz[e] intuition and the role of the subconscious to the exclusion of all else. Artistically, the basic premise of Modernism is the negation of realism. It opposes writers who deal with objective existence and encourages them rather to concentrate on the Self and the internal world of the individual . . . It is clear that the Modernist world view is one that is diametrically opposed to that of Marxism.[4]

The source of this complaint can be traced to Mao Zedong's 1942 "Talks at the Yenan Forum on Literature and Art," in which Mao had called upon writers and artists to form themselves into a "cultural army" whose proper role is to educate the masses, unite them against the feudal past, and teach them revolution. Not only are art and literature *for* the masses, according to Mao, they must be *about* them: "what is the source of all literature and art? . . . Revolutionary literature and art are the products of the reflection of the life of the people in the brains of revolutionary writers and artists. The life of the people . . . provide(s) literature and art with an inexhaustible source, their only source."[5] For Mao, there is "no such thing as art for art's sake"; all art is political. Art, to have value, must function (in terms Mao borrows from Lenin) as "cogs and wheels in the whole revolutionary machine."[6] Its power and necessity come from the fact that it can be used as a great propaganda tool, concentrating and intensifying common experiences of oppression and exploitation so as to "produce works which awaken the masses, fire them with enthusiasm and impel them to unite and struggle to transform their environment."[7] Mao has nothing but disdain for those writers who refuse to eulogize "the proletariat, the Communist Party, New Democracy and socialism" and who want to write only about themselves—they are "merely termites in the revolutionary ranks; of course, the revolutionary people have no use for these 'singers.'"[8]

If "the Modernist world view is one that is diametrically opposed to that of Marxism," then, this is because it largely rejects such Maoist criteria and creates an art that is psychologizing, subjective, sometimes surreal, an art, in short, that is rooted in the interior of the individual, and whose revolutionary, society-transforming effect comes precisely from its rejection of Mao's "proletarian revolutionary utilitarian[ism]"[9] as a satisfying definition of the arts. The selfless Buddhist ideal of the classical Chinese poet—to be empty as a mirror held up to nature—had been converted by Mao to a Marxist selflessness: "literature and art" come from "the reflection of the life of the people in the brains of revolutionary writers and artists." With a new generation of Chinese writers comes a new set of reflections in the looking glass of art: a "song," according to Bei Dao in his recent poem "Midnight Singer," is "a mirror that remembers your body," the body, that is, of the poet. After the 1989 massacre at Tiananmen Square many of these poets went into exile; now, instead of eulogizing the masses, the Party, and the government, Bei Dao writes elegies for himself and his art in an era of repressive politics—the "song" of lyric poetry may result in "the death of the singer," but that death itself is converted into a kind of immortality, as it is "pressed on a coal-black record" and "sung over and over and over."

The events at Tiananmen were to come soon enough, but during the mid-eighties there was a palpable sense of hope in the air. In spite of severe reactions from critics and from the pervasive gerontocracy (the old, accepted, Social Realist writers who dominated the Writer's Union), it did seem to be a period in which, in the Chinese phrase, a hundred flowers were to bloom and a hundred schools of thought contend. The Maoist legacy was under attack, and some critics went so far as to defend Modernism as the literary equivalent of revolution in the geopolitical sphere, suggesting that literary Modernism was in keeping with the "Four Modernizations" that are the cornerstones of Deng Xiaoping's economic and societal plan for China.[10] One critic scorned this view on the grounds that Modernism was a specific reaction to "concrete historical and social changes in the period of monopoly capitalism,"[11] and another stated outright that "just as it is impossible to talk of 'Marxist idealism' or 'Marxist Dadaism,' it is equally erroneous to advocate 'Marxist Modernism.'"[12] Though such critiques were rooted in Stalin's attack on the "bourgeois individualism" of Modernist impulses in the 1920s Soviet Union, the fact of contention, of public difference of opinion, seemed to be a good sign in a society in which this kind of dialogue had not often been possible.

Many of the Misty poets had been active in the last significant thaw in censorship of Chinese letters, the Beijing Spring of 1979, in which poets and essayists attached big-character posters to a stretch of wall in Beijing that came to be dubbed "Democracy Wall."[13] As in that earlier period—in which a multitude of unregistered and uncensored underground journals and pamphlets flourished, some of them daring to call for greater individual freedoms, for democracy, and for full literary license—1984 in China was a period of extraordinary freedom in literary debate. Earlier in the year, the novelist Ba Jin, President of the Writer's Union, gave an icebreaking speech calling for greater artistic freedom for writers. Then, at the Fourth National Writers' Congress in December 1984, Hu Qili, a senior official in the Central Committee of the Chinese Communist Party, made a speech that called for a level of freedom unimaginable in the Maoist era. He stated that writers should be allowed freedom of choice in subject and ways of expression, that freedom should prevail in literary criticism, and that "mistakes and faults in literature" should be solved through literary criticism, discussion, and debate. He said that in the past "owing to 'leftist' tendencies . . . there had been many labels pinned on writers and excessive decrees on what they should or should not write."[14] Some months later, an article in the *Worker's Daily* bemoaned the fact that "in the 10-year-long 'cultural revolution,' almost all outstanding works of art and literature were called 'poisonous weeds,' and criticized." Criticism of art and literature had lost its credibility with the people. In fact, by advertising that a work had been criticized you could make it "sell well and . . . [make] the author . . . instantly popular." The anonymous editorialist stated that this lack of credibility came from "the lingering influence of the 'leftist' way of thinking," and urged critics to "seek truth from facts" and to allow the author to reply to their critiques.[15]

When proper literature is conceived of as state-sanctioned propaganda, literary criticism becomes the act of analyzing a text for ideological merits and demerits. It is hard to express how sinister a word "criticism" is in China. Perhaps a very bad review in America will end a writer's career. Going against current literary tastes in China has often meant forced confessions, internal exile, imprisonment, torture, or being paraded through the streets with a dunce cap on and a sign with your listed crimes hung around your neck. To be "criticized" is equivalent to being politically denounced. In "Our Words," Ha Jin, a young Chinese poet who writes in English, dramatizes a case of nightmare criticism:

> Although you were the strongest boy in our neighborhood
> you could beat none of us. Whenever
> we fought with you we would shout:
> "Your father was a landlord.
> You are a bastard of a blackhearted landlord."
> Or we would mimic your father's voice
> when he was publicly denounced:
> "My name is Li Wanbao. I was a landlord;
> before liberation I exploited my hired hands
> and the poor peasants. I am guilty
> and my guilt deserves ten thousand deaths."
> Then you would withdraw your hard fists
> and flee home cursing and weeping like a wild cat.
>
> You fought only with your hands,
> but we fought with both our hands and our words.
> We fought and fought and fought
> until we overgrew you and overgrew ourselves,
> until you and we were sent to the same village
> working together in the fields
> sharing tobacco and sorghum spirits at night
> and cursing the brigade leader behind his back
> when he said: "You, petty bourgeoisie,
> must take your 're-education' seriously!"
>
> Until none of us had words.   "Our Words"

At first glance it is surprising that the new government should allow so much literary license and should try to separate literary criticism from ideology, but one must remember that China remained split between two ideological systems. For Hu Qili to criticize the hardline Marxist literary critics for a lack of objectivity was to silence some of the most vocal organs of old-school Maoism. The use of the word "leftist" as a pejorative is a key pointer that, as in the 1979 Peking Spring, centrist elements of the communist party who had taken power after Mao's death in 1976 were using the issue of literary and political freedom as a subtle attack on the previous administration.

As it turned out, the issue of freedom of debate—though politically expedient for the moment—was one that the government would drop precipitously when the climate changed, as it had before, when the Beijing Spring of 1979 was suppressed. At that time, when Deng Xiaoping's government felt that they were beginning to lose control of the tenor of the debate on Democracy Wall and in the journals, and when several thousand workers—who had been "sent down to the countryside" in a Cultural Revolution campaign designed to make urban youth learn rural values—staged a protest in Beijing, the government cracked down, outlawing the underground journals and making examples of several high-profile individuals. The essayist Wei Jingsheng, founder of the journal *Exploration*, had repeatedly called for democracy and greater individualism, and had exposed the maltreatment of political prisoners in Beijing prisons. In March 1979, he was tried, convicted, and sentenced to fifteen years in jail, where he has been kept in isolation for years at a time and has been so malnourished that he has lost his hair and teeth.[16] He remains in prison today.

This crackdown came to be called the Anti-Spiritual Pollution Campaign, and it had its victims among the critical defenders of the Misty poets as well. The critics who bucked against Maoist criteria by defending the new poetry suffered for their outspokenness. The nail that sticks up gets hammered down, says the Japanese proverb; for sticking up for the Misty poets the critic Xu Jingya was forced to publish a "self-criticism" in which he repudiated his earlier article and promised to "examine [himself] carefully, to eradicate the influence of capitalist liberalism, and to keep forever in the forefront of [his] mind the socialist orientation in literature and art."[17] Similarly, the critic Sun Shaozhen was forced to recant an article in which he defended the Misty poets, an article that became the focus of an organized campaign of criticism, with over a hundred articles written in rebuttal between 1981 and 1986.

This pendulum swing from expression to repression is a prime topos of Chinese politics since the Revolution. The Hundred Flowers Campaign of 1957 (another brief period during which open literary and political dissent was tolerated) was quickly followed by the repressive Anti-Rightist Campaign; the Beijing Spring died into the winter of the Anti-Spiritual Pollution Campaign; and the remarkable toleration of political and esthetic difference that characterized China during my stay there gave way in turn to another campaign of repression—the Anti-Bourgeois Liberalization Campaign. This perpetual cycling from expression to repression and back again crops up in poet after poet in allegories of the seasons; Yang Lian, for example, states in "Sowing" that "storms may have whipped [him] in the past," but that he has faith in "the coming hope of spring / and of the next sure harvest." For some among the more pessimistic generation of poets who followed the Misty poets, a generation Michelle Yeh has labeled the "Post-Misty" poets, nature is less benevolent; for Fei Ye, for example, "Each day and night is a season in hell" ("The Curse"), and the alienation of government and populace is figured forth in a parallel alienation between nature's forces and humanity: "Dark thunderclouds grumble distantly, / Random message sent to a small planet / By a god living on a far off star" ("We Are Little Creatures on a Little Planet").

In any case, Big Brother seemed not to be watching in 1984, and in the absence of his gaze those persistent hundred flowers blossomed again. Of course it was only a matter of time before they would be labeled poisonous weeds and mowed down once more, but this time the consequences would seriously shake up the communist system from top to bottom. Perhaps as a consequence of the perceived loosening of government restrictions, 1985 developed into a year of barely suppressed unrest on Beijing campuses, of protests by former Red Guards who had gone down to the countryside in Shaanxi in the Cultural Revolution and now wanted permission to return to Beijing, and of a remarkable outpouring of cynical dissidence in literature, music, painting and film.[18] When this unrest broke out into prodemocracy demonstrations in 1987 (in Beijing, Tianjin, and Nanjing) the government responded with bans, with vilification of "bourgeois liberalization," by dismissing the activist physicist Fang Lizhi from his position at Beijing University, and by purging the popular journalist Liu Binyan from the party. Though for the moment a cap had been put on student pressures for political reform, a mere two years later the Democracy Movement resurfaced in force. In the summer of 1989 many journalists were in Beijing to cover the historic upcoming visit of Mikhail Gorbachev to Beijing. Through satellite uplinks, the world watched as massive demonstrations of millions of students and workers took place in Tiananmen Square. In a protracted standoff with the government, the students staged hunger strikes and blocked police and army units from reclaiming the square through passive resistance, and Beijing artists erected a massive plaster "Goddess of Democracy" statue as a new monument in the square while the government, in part because of the timing, looked on helplessly. On the night of June 3, however, the army moved in; troops fired at will into the milling crowds; tanks crushed the barricades and those unlucky enough to fall before them, killing over seven hundred students and workers, and injuring thousands more. By the end of June 4, the movement was decisively crushed.

I had been living in Beijing only a few months when one of my students, knowing that I was a poet and was anxious to meet the new Chinese poets, took me aside and told me that his brother-in-law happened to be a poet, and would I like to meet him? This was my introduction to the Misty poets and their younger imitators. My father and I had come to China together, were teaching in the same university, and had already set up a translation workshop in our flat in the heavily ornate yet run-down Friendship Hotel complex, where we lived in benign captivity with other "Foreign Experts," with guards at the gate to keep China out and with restaurants, theaters, and sports facilities to make us feel better about being kept in. We had been working on the poems of Wang Wei, the Tang Dynasty poet of court life and of Buddhist retreat in the country, but soon, in spite of the guards' intimidation, our rooms were crowded with young, passionate, bombastic poets and editors declaiming the end of Social Realism, alternately praising and dismissing their contemporaries, telling horror stories of the Cultural Revolution, and excitedly combing through my rock-and-roll tapes. It was the new breath of Chinese poetry that had blown tumultuously into our rooms: at once dogmatic and irreverent, ironic yet sentimental, obscure and yet pierced through with the clarity of a diamond in a glass of water.

Where had these poets, apparently without a breath of Classical Chinese poetry in them, come from? The literary history of this new school has not yet been written, but something can be pieced together. Duo Duo was among the first to start writing the new poetry. He began creating strange, surreal, often absurd, and sometimes terrifying poetic landscapes during that culminating absurdity, the Great Proletarian Cultural Revolution (1966–1976):

> Songs, but the bloody revolution goes unnoticed
> August is a ruthless bow
> The vicious son walks out of the farmhouse
> Bringing with him tobacco and a dry throat
> The beasts must bear cruel blinders
> Corpses encrusted in hair hang

From the swollen drums of their buttocks
Till the sacrifices behind the fence
Become blurry
From far away there comes marching a troop
Of smoking people

"When People Rise from Cheese, Statement #1"

His idiosyncratic style often consists of a surreal juxtaposition of vignettes that create a cumulative mood or meaning. With Duo Duo's poetry the reading experience becomes one of deciphering common themes in poems that veer wildly through space and time and narrative—the reader must find the mathematical constant that unifies the set. This can make his poetry among the most obscure, or "misty," of the poets presented here, but one must understand that in poetry that often edges into dissidence a certain slipperiness is a survival trait in contemporary China. In this poem, one of his more instantly readable ones, he sketches out a horrifying landscape that seems to come out of Bosch or Goya, an Orwellian *Animal Farm* where vicious farmers torture their herd and the farmyard is a place of bloody revolution and sacrifice. But in the enigmatic conclusion Duo Duo might be suggesting a bit of hope: "From far away there comes marching a troop / Of smoking people." What the approaching generation coming out of the smoke signifies is itself misty, but it could be that, like the Misty poets, the new generation is here to offer a break from a past of nightmare politics.

In a key Misty manifesto published in *Today* (*Jintian*), an unknown author, who took the pseudonym Hong Huang, sketched out some of the esthetic principles of this loosely-knit school. He saw the new poetry as a product of a new national spirit, a new generation whose decisive break from the past is to abandon the strict form of classical Chinese poetry, and to reject both state-controlled ideological content and proletarian realism, the preferred mode in poetry before the Misties:

This breakthrough in content has led to a breakthrough in form. Now that the poet's own wealth of authentic feeling has replaced an abstract, false and preju-diced set of "intents" as poetic material; now that a truly vital self, one endowed with dignity, intellect and a complex inner life, has appeared in poetry; now that poetry is no longer hack literature, no longer the mouthpiece of politics; now that we are standing face to face with this land imbued with suffering and yet full of hope, musing on this sorrowful but radiant dawn; we need our own stance, our own voice.[19]

Consider, if only for the sake of contrast, some of the propaganda that served as poetry prior to the Misties. Here, for example, is a small Cultural Revolution poem by Wu Shuteh:

The moon follows the earth,
The earth follows the sun,
Oil follows our steps,
And we shall always follow the Communist Party.

"We Shall Always Follow the Party"[20]

And here are lines by the well-known poet Guo Mo-ro:

II

The people are industrious and courageous:
Enforce national defense, revolutionize traditions.
Strong is the leadership of our Communist government,
Herald of the proletariat.
    Industrialization, rainbowlike atmosphere;
    Tillers own their lands, earth belongs to all.
    May our glorious fatherland
    Steadily advance to Utopia.

from "In Praise of New China"[21]

In the past two decades a new vision has appeared in Chinese poetry, a vision reinforced by the many translations of European Symbolists and American Modernists that poured out after Mao's death. These are poets who are well read in Western poetics as well as Western poetry. In seeking a way to revitalize the Chinese poem, to discover a usable past in Chinese literature, the author of the Misty manifesto paid particular attention to what Ezra Pound and T. E. Hulme had to say about Chinese poetics:

We should revive the rich visual-imagist tradition of Chinese poetry, what Hulme called a "visual, concrete language," and oppose external logic and syntax as the sole source of poetic creation. The American imagist poet Ezra Pound wrote: "It is . . . because certain Chinese poets have been content to set forth their matter without moralizing and without comment that one labours to make a translation."[22]

Although the Misty poets diverge from the Imagists in many respects, particularly in their occasional embracing of large rootless abstractions with no objective correlative in sight, in other respects the comparison is apt, particularly in the case of Gu Cheng's early poems and in Shu Ting's uses of parataxis. Like the Imagists, Hong Huang espoused a break from rhyme, a substitution of "irregular lines for ornate parallelism," and "form . . . [as] simply an extension of content."[23] He was also particularly drawn to Pound's criterion of poetry that accomplishes its task "without moralizing and without comment," since his task at hand was to make a case for poetry that is a mirror for the individual, not for society, to free poetry from bludgeoning rhetoric and allow it to draw its form neither from handed-down traditional forms nor from an external map of ideology, but from the associative process of the individual mind.

A thread of Eastern vision had entered the West through early translations of Japanese haiku, through Arthur Waley and through Pound's endlessly popular *Cathay*. Stitched through Imagism, "Amygism," Vorticism, and Objectivism, it was a key pointer from the Romantic poetics of declaration to the modern poetics of suggestion. It is a culminating irony that this very thread, stitched back again through translation, should help to revitalize a century of stagnant Chinese poetics.

But other Western elements have also taken root in this poetry, not all of them Modernist. Sometimes the parallel juxtapositioning of traditional Chinese poetry mutates into the wild associations of Surrealism, the anarchistic buffoonery of Dada, or the fragmented, repetitive, Cubist surfaces of Stein or Pierre Reverdy. Some lines in these poems seem lifted directly out of Romanticism or Symbolism, with their use of the pathetic fallacy, their personification of elements of nature, and their willingness to let the symbol stand for the thing. Yet this merely makes them all the more modern, for the innovations of the American Modernists are incorrectly understood as a complete rejection of Romanticism: Eliot's "Prufrock," Williams's "Pastoral," Stevens's "Snow Man" (to choose from countless examples) were largely attempts to find ways to make the poetry of the immediate past new—by ironizing it, urbanizing it, by reinventing the relation between humanity and nature. Like the Western Modernist poetry to which they owe so much, the Chinese Modernists are writing a hybrid poetry, a poetry that derives its power and interest through being a poetry of transition. These are poems written by a lost generation that is writing at a time of radical shifts in ideology.

A much-quoted passage from *A Farewell To Arms* illustrates the sense of exploded ideals that Hemingway's generation felt after the senseless slaughter of World War I:

I was always embarrassed by the words sacred, glorious, and sacrifice and the expression in vain. We had heard them, sometimes standing in the rain almost out of earshot, so that only the shouted words came through, and had read them, on proclamations that were slapped up by billposters over other proclamations, now for a long time, and I had seen nothing sacred, and the things that were glorious had no glory and the sacrifices were like the stockyards in Chicago if nothing was done with the meat except to bury it. . . . Abstract words such as glory, honor, courage, or hallow were obscene beside the concrete names of villages, the numbers of roads, the names of rivers, the numbers of regiments and the dates."[24]

We see this same resistance to ideology and rhetoric among the new Chinese poets. They are of a generation reared since early childhood on the economics of Marxism and "Mao Zedong Thought," yet with the death of Mao and the fall of the Gang of Four, China quickly shifted away from the command economy of state capitalism toward a demand economy and increased privatization in production and marketing. These changes, of course, necessitated a radical re-education of the population, to the point of questioning whether Marxist analyses, rooted in the economics of early industrial capitalism, were still relevant in an era of worldwide markets. This unprecedented ideological shift produced, if anything, a greater cynicism in the population regarding government proclamations than had been present before.

Caught between ideological systems, and disappointed with a government that still runs a command economy with regard to cultural products, these poets are deeply skeptical; as Bei Dao says in his poem "Answer," "Listen. *I don't believe!*" He doesn't believe that China's rejection of the Maoist legacy will translate into freedom: "They say the Ice Age ended years ago," he says, then "Why are there icicles everywhere?" Like Hemingway, he won't believe anything the world tells him: "I don't believe the sky is blue. / I don't believe what the thunder says." Yet, as we will see later, Bei Dao's "answer," like Hemingway's, is not only one of rejection, but is also a search for something new to believe in, in a world drained of meaning. It is a vital engagement with the possibility of cultural, as opposed to economic, renewal.

These attempts at comparative poetics are simplifications, of course; the game of influence is a *Through the Looking Glass* one where the ball isn't merely batted around, but tends to get up and walk away, and where all the players have a tendency to turn into something else. "Every age is a pigeon hole," says Wallace Stevens; certainly the Misty poets themselves, both in conversation and in writing, resist being pigeonholed as resulting from a set of influences.

Thus, in part because "the most severe accusation levelled against the New Poetry is that it is too Westernized,"[25] it was important for Hong Huang (even as he rejected classical Chinese form) to show that the Misties are, properly seen, a product of Chinese tradition. He insisted that the new poets should revive the ambiguity, the many levels of meaning that are "the essence of the classical tradition in Chinese poetry," but, though "this may coincide with contemporary Western poetics . . . it is certainly not worshipping and fawning on things foreign."[26] And it is true as well that, to some extent, the development of Misty poetry might owe something to the already extant Modernist traditions in Chinese poetry—the work of the Crescent School in prerevolutionary China and the Modernist Taiwanese poets of the postrevolutionary period. This innovative work was not celebrated when the Misty poets took their first step toward Modernism at the end of the Cultural Revolution (though it is currently undergoing a new vogue), but it was *available* to those who tried hard enough to get it, in editions from Hong Kong and Taiwan that found their way into China. I haven't heard these poets speak of the earlier traditions as strong influences, though; perhaps this is in part a question of territoriality—along with Modernist poetics, these writers have embraced the Modernist infatuation with innovation and genius, a quantity that the presence of these earlier Modernists threatens to subvert.

Of course, the earlier Chinese Modernists were themselves a reaction to exposure to the Western tradition and had been criticized as solipsistic and bourgeois, so that claiming them as forebears wouldn't have effectively countered the all-too-familiar criticism of Western influence (which at various times has taken the names "rightist," "spiritual pollution," and "bourgeois liberalization"). But it is interesting to see that after fending off the question of influence as best he can in his essay, Hong Huang came back to his real stance—the poet must face both Chinese and Western traditions with self-reliance, rejecting what is no longer seen as useful, and appropriating whatever can give poetry its power back again:

We live in an era of world cultural interfusion. The magnificent heritage of Eastern classical painting, drama and poetry has influenced the modern Western arts. Similarly, in drawing on the modern arts of the Western world, we can come to understand more deeply the true value of our own artistic tradition; we can combine this tradition more harmoniously with the content of modern life in order to develop our own new literature and art. Perhaps this is the secret of the New Poetry of the new Chinese generation, a secret which our poets and critics refuse to take seriously.[27]

This stance—a rejection of the immediate past of poetic realism combined with a respect for the broader tradition of Chinese literature, as well as a certain defensiveness about the Western tradition combined with a self-reliant sense of what can be learned from it—is common to these poets. As Yang Lian says, "tradition is an eternal present; to neglect it is to neglect ourselves";[28] however, "we must pick out from the numerous and diverse sources the 'inner core' that is still strong and vital; this is the vitality and strength that Yeats called mature wisdom."[29]

Bei Dao, the most popular of these poets, is in some ways the most mutable in his use of form and genre. "Night: Theme and Variations" utilizes a poetics of listing, of juxtaposed vignettes, to create a cumulative meditation on power and privacy in which the dusty dream of an imperial past is contrasted with a rude modern world in which people line up like fences and the lonely interiors of the new people are searched by blinding streetlights. The scene is seen by an invisibly present sympathetic intelligence, who collates the desperate lives of cat and tramp and truck driver with a pyrotechnic beauty—headlight beams probing the darkness, colorful neon, and the water's trembling light. It is a poem in which "roads converge": the present and the past, the powerful and the disenfranchised, haunt each other and resonate together in this beautiful and subtly threatening poem with the ghost peals of a bell struck by moonlight.

Bei Dao brings this bittersweet intelligence to many brief lyrics, some more than others admitting the possibility of redemption. In "Sweet Tangerines" a world that is wrecked and bitter can almost be saved by those small, bright, balled-up bits of sun:

> The oranges are ripe.
> Bitter threads web every
> sun-drenched segment.
>   Let me
> walk into your heart to gather
> my dismembered dream.   *from* "The Oranges Are Ripe"

But the world of Bei Dao's poetry is as radically unstable as Chinese politics, a place where such dreams easily switch into nightmare, as in the poem of that title, where the worst visions of the unconscious fail to match the horror of the world's waking dream:

> On the shifting wind
> I painted an eye
> then the blocked moment passed
> but no one awoke
> the nightmare still overflowed in the sunshine
> spilling across the river bed, creeping over the cobbles
> provoking new friction and strife
> in the branches, on the eaves
> the birds' frightened gazes froze into ice
> and dropped to earth
> then a thin layer of frost
> formed over the ruts in the road
> no one awoke   "Nightmare"

Clearly Bei Dao is opposed to the unnamed horror that we glimpse in this poem, but, characteristically, he wreathes its ultimate meaning, personal, political, in a fog of symbols. However, in his well-known poem "Declaration" he comes out into the open, declaring himself a dissident: "I will not kneel on the ground / allowing the executioners to look tall / the better to obstruct the wind of freedom." In "Answer" he is even clearer. In a corrupt and dangerous world where scoundrels carry their "baseness around like an ID card" and honor becomes an epitaph, the poet declares himself on the side of political victims:

> Listen. *I don't believe!*
> OK. You've trampled
> a thousand enemies underfoot. Call me
> a thousand and one.   *from* "Answer"

The poet here is writing a national poetry, not one of nationalism, but one in which the poet becomes a ritual sacrifice in the midst of cataclysm, purifying the corrupt nation through the sacrifice of his own body. "If the sea should break through the sea-wall," he says, "let its brackish water fill my heart."

In the complexly associative last stanza, the spinning stars suggest the wheeling of the day, then are compared to the ancient pictographs that have evolved into the language of the poem, and, finally, become the watching eyes of the coming generation—aspects of present, past, and future all wound into one symbol:

> The earth revolves. A glittering constellation
> pricks the vast defenseless sky.
> Can you see it there? that ancient ideogram—
> the eye of the future, gazing back.   *from* "Answer"

Prophesies of the future, signs of present cataclysm, and the needs of the generation that follows—that these become conflated with Chinese pictographs suggests at least the possibility that poetry can show a way out of today's repression.

But since the events at Tiananmen Square, in exile from China, Bei Dao's pessimism seems to have triumphed, at least temporarily. In "The Morning's Story," written as China fell into the grip of yet another round of torture, indiscriminate detentions, and trials of political dissidents, and as the official press sought to deny the extent and nature of the Tiananmen Square Massacre, words, newspapers, and books became the weapons used to stifle freedom of thought and expression: "A word has abolished another word / a book has issued orders / to burn another book." And yet this very repression serves to link together those who, like Bei Dao, *"don't believe."* Consider these lines from "Requiem," his poem written for the victims of the massacre at Tiananmen:

Not your bodies but your souls
shall share a common birthday every year
You are all the same age
love has founded for the dead
an everlasting alliance
you embrace each other closely
in the massive register of deaths

During the hopeful days of Democracy Wall and the 1979 Beijing Spring—the forerunner to the Democracy Movement of 1989—Bei Dao co-edited the underground journal *Today* (*Jintian*) with his friend Mang Ke. In the intervening years Bei Dao found himself receiving widespread international attention and some measure of domestic success. Mang Ke, on the other hand, has remained on the outside looking in, publishing his books primarily in mimeographed copies (what the Russians call *samizdat*). He is a poet of sexuality and morbidity, of bitterness and tenderness facing the world. In a poem like "To Children" one can best feel the generous, generative side of the man:

I'm just an ordinary man,
but I think of
giving you myself
Grow on my body
Let my heart be sucked empty
by your powerful roots and stems   *from* "To Children"

Before his poetry developed into the devastating sophistication and profoundly cynical denunciation of humanity of his latest work, the epic "Ape Herd," Mang Ke wrote a number of early, allegorical protest poems such as "Sunflower in the Sun." Here, he uses natural metaphor as a screen to hide his powerful indictment of political repression, utilizing the common Cultural Revolution identification of Mao Zedong with the sun and of the masses with the sunflowers that follow its course through the sky.

Do you see it
see the sunflower raising its head
facing down the sun
Its head eclipsing the sun
The sun is gone
but the sunflower is radiant   *from* "Sunflower in the Sun"

Mang Ke, who, like so many others, spent the Cultural Revolution being "re-educated," doing labor in the countryside, reverses the propagandists' symbol to show that before his death, Mao, elevated to near-godhead, had become alienated from the people, had become a cruel god that the people no longer cared to worship. When the media, from journalism to high art, is controlled by the government, that simple thing, metaphor, becomes vitally political, with a potential for harm as great as the use of political euphemism and bureaucratese that Orwell deplored in "Politics in the English Language." In our own culture, as party spin-doctors twist the facts for partisan purposes and simplify complex issues into easily remembered "sound-bites," as the mass media relays military terms like "collateral damage" to the public as a euphemism for the death of civilians in the carpet-bombing of Iraq, and as advertisers use parataxis and metonymy to coat their products with a glaze of glamour, sex, and power, we should be alert to the ways in which the powerful language of poetry can be appropriated to manipulate public opinion. For the poets to step into the breach and try to reclaim metaphor from the political hacks is a dangerous act, and a praiseworthy one. As Orwell wrote,

political language—and with variations this is true of all political parties, from Conservatives to Anarchists—is designed to make lies sound truthful and murder respectable, and to give an appearance of solidity to pure wind. One cannot change this all in a moment, but one can at least change one's own habits, and from time to time one can, if one jeers loudly enough, send some worn-out and useless phrase . . . into the dustbin where it belongs.[30]

The attempt to undermine political rhetoric and metaphor is present throughout these poems. Yang Lian, as we will see later, does an extended attack on "the sun" in his poem cycle "Nuorilang," as does Mang Ke in his long poem "Ape Herd." Paradoxically, it is their reaction against the politicization of poetic language that most unifies these poets, much as contemporary attacks on freedom of expression in America—from right-wing attempts to censor Robert Mappelthorpe and Two Live Crew to leftist attempts to censor offensive speech on college campuses—have unified creative artists of every stamp.

These poets are attempting to create a counterculture, a poetry of dissenting opinion to counter the government's monolithic presentation of history. Consider, for example, Gu Cheng's elegy for the Red Guards buried in a graveyard at Shapingba Park. Comparing the "burrs and beggars' lice, / ants and lizards" infesting the graves of the Red Guards killed during the Cultural Revolution to the "fresh flowers" placed on the graves of the Revolutionary Martyrs (who fought in the 1949 revolution) at nearby Geyue Shan, Gu Cheng is contrasting popular sentiment toward these two incidents of Mao Zedong-led revolution. During the Great Proletarian Cultural Revolution, Mao Zedong, who had been losing power and status to more centrist leaders, such as Deng Xiaoping, called on the new generation to organize into Red Guard brigades and to take revolution to the streets, attacking the entrenched bureaucracy of the Party and elements of the Imperial past. At a time when America was going through a different sort of countercultural youth revolution, the Chinese youth were unleashed upon the nation with a particular fury.

> Everybody knew
> it was the Sun who led you,
> to the tune of a marching song,
> off to Paradise.
> Later, halfway there
> you tired, tripped
> over a bed whose frame was inlaid
> with stars and bullet holes.
> It had seemed to you
> a game, a game to play   *from* "Forever Parted: Graveyard"

During this period, more than four thousand monasteries in occupied Tibet were looted, their great wealth dumped into the Brahmaputra, or burned, and then the massive structures were dynamited, effectively destroying the cultural past of one of the world's oldest civilizations. Paradoxically, many cultural artifacts have survived that period only because international smugglers, disguising themselves as Red Guards, joined in the looting and then smuggled prayer wheels, manuscripts, paintings, and statues into neighboring Nepal. But the Red Guards were betrayed by Mao when he felt that he could no longer control them. He sent the army against them in 1967 to gain control over them, killing thousands of Red Guards in confrontations across China, and sent millions into internal exile in Tibet, Xinjiang, and Qinghai.

"Forever Parted" participates in the new genre of "Scar Literature," the outpouring of exposés of Cultural Revolution atrocities that flourished with the intermittent relative loosening of restrictions on literary production that prevailed in China after Mao, at least until the June 4th massacre in 1989. On the one hand, Gu Cheng identifies with the rebellious youth brigades ("I don't have an older brother / but I believe you / are my older brother"); on the other hand, his elegy for them acknowledges their crimes, how they tortured people like children unthinkingly torturing birds and insects:

> who pulled the golden feathers from
> the reed finch's wing,
> spattering the whole earth
> with tiny drops of blood,
> or teased the borer beetle

with bounds and flame
and forced him to totter
across a window sill stage
for the crime of eating wood chips?

from "Forever Parted: Graveyard"

The absurdity of the borer beetle's crime, and the harshness of his punish-
ment, were the merest commonplaces of the Cultural Revolution, during
which thousands of intellectuals and others were beaten to death and many
others chose to avoid persecution through the only recourse available to
them—suicide. Like the borer beetle, Deng Xiaoping's son was thrown
from a window by Red Guards and left for dead, his body paralyzed. It
was in part because Deng Xiaoping and his family shared the persecution
of the Cultural Revolution that he was able to emerge after Mao's death
as China's leader. Unfortunately, this proved to be no guarantee that he
would avoid the mistakes of the past—after all, he was strongly involved
in the purging of hundreds of thousands during the 1957 Anti-Rightist
Campaign, and in 1989 he gave the order for the People's Liberation Army
to massacre hundreds of demonstrating civilians in Tiananmen Square.

It is hard to give a period of such profound turmoil a human face.
History, a thing of numbers and general movements, effaces the human
equation. A period of widespread starvation followed on Mao's Great
Leap Forward in which at least twenty million died. To understand it I
think of a friend who told me how the people of her village were so hun-
gry that they boiled and ate insects, along with roots, grass, and the leaves
of trees, until the countryside for miles around was barren. When I try to
comprehend the absurdity of the crimes for which people were persecuted
during the Cultural Revolution, I think of a colleague who was severely
beaten and humiliated by Red Guards, then paraded through the streets
wearing a dunce cap, for writing an essay on Shelley's "Ode to the West
Wind." The excuse for his persecution: Mao had stated in a speech against
the capitalist West that the "east wind prevails over the west wind." Our
friend's scholarly essay was not an attempt to reverse the dominant meta-
phors of Chinese politics like Mang Ke's "Sunflower in the Sun," but this
mattered not at all to those who vilified him. I think also of a British officer
I met in a hostel in Nepal, commander of a troop of Ghurka soldiers, who
was stationed on the border of China and Hong Kong during the Cultural
Revolution. Although refugees who made it to Hong Kong spread tales
of horror, the direct evidence of it came floating daily out of China on its
rivers—corpses, sometimes twenty at once, chained together and thrown
into the water to drown.

For creative writers it was a time of great repression as well. The first writer I met in China was a poet who had spent twenty years in Qinghai Province (the Siberia of China) after being labeled a "rightist" (along with 300,000 other intellectuals) in the 1957 Anti-Rightist Campaign. Although in internal exile for his writing, he continued creating manuscripts that he knew he would be unable to publish, in the hope that some day the pendulum might swing back from repression to expression. During the Cultural Revolution, though, his flat was searched in a series of raids by Red Guards who burned all his books and manuscripts. When Mao finally died in 1976 he found himself in the position of being a writer with nothing to show, outside of memory, for a quarter century's writing. I asked him if he was frightened to write about his experiences during the Cultural Revolution, in case China should shift to the left again and his statements be used against him. He paused, then said, firmly, "No. Once you've been to hell, you're not afraid of going there again."

A certain complacency or smugness is always a temptation when dealing with poetry that can be classified as dissident, protest poetry, or poetry of exile. It is easy to deplore another nation's policies, harder to have perspective on one's own. In the past of polarized cold war politics, the eloquence of a Solzhenitsyn or a Brodsky was rightly lauded by the American literary establishment; yet would international recognition of these truly excellent writers have come as quickly if their example had not affirmed our own political system? I think a wiser perspective is to view such tales of censorship not in a spirit of self-congratulation, but as a warning. As I write this, a newly conservative Supreme Court is engaged in rolling back civil rights legislation, already having weakened prisoners' Miranda rights, allowed the police to use "fruit of the poison tree" confessions (thus encouraging police brutality), and circumscribed the scope of 4th Amendment protection against unreasonable search and seizure. Only now, as we go to press, has the free-speech right of doctors to discuss abortion with their patients in federally funded clinics been restored. The military in its past three engagements—Grenada, Panama, and Iraq—has limited the press's access to the action and to information, organizing reporters into pools to limit independent investigative journalism, and has engaged in extensive disinformation campaigns in order to demonize the enemy (the most ludicrous example: Noriega's refrigerator was said to be packed with bags of cocaine—though they were later admitted to contain tamales). The press itself no longer fits its own self-myth as an objective relayer of facts, a fourth estate owned by a scattering of spunky independents, which checks the excesses of the rich and powerful for the common person. Now the "independent" press is largely owned by a few megacorporations.

Of course, all this is the news of the moment, liable to change in the next moment into "old news," perhaps even before this book sees print. In *Walden* Thoreau is upset with the news for reporting only sensational tragedies, "one house burned, or one vessel wrecked, or one steamboat blown up, or one cow run over on the Western railroad," while ignoring essential principles; thus he asserts that "To a philosopher all *news*, as it is called, is gossip, and they who edit and read it are old women over their tea."[31] If, therefore, the specifics shift and mutate by the time you pick up this book, think of the principle that lies behind them. As I write we are, like China, on a pendulum swing from expression back to repression. Of course, while these political and economic attacks on civil rights and free speech are grave, they are not of the same level of murderous repression as that which led to the Tiananmen Square Massacre, or even of our own past of Jim Crow laws, blacklisting, back-alley abortions, and political witch-hunts. However, the Chinese example (and our own regressions) should be a warning not to assume our own freedoms as innocent, enduring facts—their survival depends precisely on how vigilant, or how complacent, we are.

The poet whose work will seem most familiar to the Western audience is Shu Ting. Her themes are romance and loss—and her poetics may seem antiquated to the postmodern sensibility. But this merely shows up one of the prime problems of translation—one can translate the words, and one can translate the spirit, but one can't translate the historical moment that made those particular words written in that way so revolutionary. Shu Ting has opened the field in modern Chinese poetry to include romance, emotion, and love. To understand why this is important, one has to remember that during the Cultural Revolution sexuality and romance were strictly taboo topics in the national and literary media. Mao had explicitly stated that those impulses were to be redirected toward revolution; Jonathan Spence sees this sexual repression (combined with perpetual supervision and revolutionary sacrifice) as an element that led the Chinese Red Guard youth to "perform countless acts of calculated sadism" on their elders.[32] For a woman to dramatize her love life simply and emotionally, to express the loss of her mother and her yearnings for past lovers, was to put a crack in the dam of a nation's emotional repression:

> I'm afraid to display these tokens of love,
> though I've written many odes
>   to flowers, to the sea, to daybreak.
> A gentle, deep yearning for you,

mother,
not cascading, not a waterfall,
but an ancient well, drowned with bushes and flowers,
singing in silence.

from "Mother"

Hers is poetry intricately involved with nature as well as emotion. Like Wordsworth in *The Prelude*, claiming that his blank verse form came from a river's "steady cadence," a "ceaseless music" which "compos'd [his] thoughts" (Book I, lines 279–281), Shu Ting claims in "The Gift" that "Everything I feel / is a gift from the earth." The processes of nature are converted into a natural poetry that speaks through her: "Falling and budding leaves / compose thousands of lines," she says in "Falling Leaves," and in "The Gift" she becomes a migratory bird whose "bloody wings / will brush out one intense line of verse / to pierce all souls and time." What makes her poetry surpass that of her imitators, though, is her sure sure sense of atmosphere, her lyrical precision, and the parallelisms that at times structure her poetry into something like Classical Chinese *lu shi*:

The eucalyptus wood swirls.
Stars above teem into a kaleidoscope.
On a rusty anchor,
eyes mirror the dizzy sky.

Holding up a book to shade the candle
and with a finger in between the lips,
I sit in an eggshell quiet,
having a semi-transparent dream.

from "Two or Three Incidents Recollected"

It is remarkable how easily she shifts from intensely private, Dickinsonian exploration of the interior to an outward-directed poetry in which she becomes a representative woman, breaking China's emotional chains through her own example. In "Motherland, Dear Motherland" (a poem not included here) she *becomes* China in the way Whitman contains multitudes, at once individual and *en masse*: "I am one billionth of you; / your millions of square acres in me." But she is not always generatively optimistic and patriotic. In "Perhaps," one of her most political poems, written just before the "Beijing Spring," she questions the role of the poet in the new society: "Perhaps our hearts / will have no reader." And yet this societal deadness to the needs of the heart is a call to selfless action:

Perhaps we can only protest others' suffering
silent to our own misfortune
Perhaps

because this call is irresistable
we have no other choice   *from* "Perhaps"

It is a similar role that Jiang He, the most relentlessly political of these writers, sees for the poet—spokesperson, martyr, the representative human whose personal suffering is iconic of the political and emotional repression of a nation:

I am nailed to death on the prison wall;
like a flag rising my clothes slowly drift.

from "Unfinished Poem"

In Jiang He's "A Date with Execution" the poet dramatizes the day of his own execution: "Handcuffs and shackles burrow into my flesh, / whips and blood weave a net on my body . . . I was born in darkness to bring light / and they must kill me to hide their lies." The poet speaks for the repressed and, in this powerful poem, represents his own torture and death to show his solidarity with victims of political repression throughout history:

There is a wild gathering of people
deprived of light, darkly packed;
I also stand in this crowd.
I am every person who has died by the ancient
     methods of torture.
I look sadly
on my own execution,
my blood gushing until I am dry.   *from* "A Date with Execution"

Like Bei Dao, Jiang He sets himself apart as a dissident, identifying himself with Bei Dao's redeemer of a corrupt society, its representative victim. We see this common thread in his poetry developed most powerfully in the poem "Memorial," a long meditation on the memorial buildings on Tiananmen Square, the location of the Museum of History, the Great Hall of the People, and the Gate of Heavenly Peace that breaks the high red walls of the Forbidden City and where a giant portrait of Mao still presides over the square. In this poem the body of the poet is "built of piled stones"; he becomes a countermemorial, a memorial to repression and to the death of students and workers on Tiananmen and on the surrounding streets: "Here, right here / I have been sold so many times. / Beheaded / my body, bearing still the traces of the chains, / just so, was I buried." In a famous statement Mao had said that "power comes from the barrel of a gun," and Jiang He laments that: "the truth that curses could not speak / was left to the mouths of the guns." In the simple and touching conclusion he offers another version of truth:

Well then
it is struggle that's my theme
my poems, my life
I offer up:
Memorial.   *from* "Memorial"

In comparison, Ha Jin's dramatic monologue, "An Old Red Guard's Reply," is a despairing testament to a wasted past:

Having been deceived again and again
nobody could care whether there is any truth.
Try to persuade us,
portraying the magnificent deeds of the old days
or promising us a golden monument in the archives.

from "An Old Red Guard's Reply"

Like Jiang He, Ha Jin contrasts two monuments, the "golden monument" that is promised to celebrate revolutionary heroes, versus the Red Guards themselves, living monuments to the inaction and the moral paralysis that come from being deceived too many times ("Having been wrecked so many times / we will not set sail once more").

Though some of the poets discussed here embrace the role of dissident or political victim, others have been forced into political prominence against their will. Czeslaw Milosz, in his comments at the 1990 inaugural reading of the new organization Chinese Writers in Exile, spoke of his solidarity with them and defined his own relation to politics: "I am by nature a hermetic poet, but history has been thrust upon me." Although some of the poets presented here are apolitical, history has been thrust upon others with a particular vengeance. Fei Ye has spent time in Chinese prisons, and Mang Ke was arrested briefly after the Tiananmen Square massacre; a number of the others, who happened to be attending a conference overseas at the time of the crackdown in Tiananmen Square, have become poets of exile. Bei Dao is in Norway where he has brought the journal *Today* back to life; Zhang Zhen lives in Sweden, though she is currently studying at the University of Iowa; Gu Cheng is in New Zealand, Duo Duo in Denmark, Jiang He, Chou Ping, and Ha Jin are in America, and Bei Ling is poet-in-residence at Brown University. Fei Ye, who moved to a run-down section of Berkeley some years before the 1989 Democracy Movement, is perhaps the saddest case here; after recurrent problems with Chinese officials he was allowed to leave China to join his wife in America, where he founded the organization Chinese Writers in Exile. He is currently serving a five-year sentence in California for assault. The remaining poets, to the best of my knowledge, are still in China.

In Yang Lian's poetry we see themes common to much of the new generation, but his involvement with history and myth gives his work a special strength. In "An Ancient Children's Tale," from his series "Bell on the Frozen Lake," the poet's memories are expanded to include the whole of Chinese history. In this beautifully crafted piece, he presents a montage of Chinese history, handicraft, ornamentation, architecture, and trade, yet shows, in the middle stanza, a developing class difference, contrasting "the glazed and opulent palaces . . . the bloody red / walls, and . . . the people rapt in luxurious dreams / for centuries in their incense-filled chambers" with "a village girl [who] wander[s] down to the river, / her eyes so clear and bright with grief." In the final stanza this leads to war and revolution:

> In the end, smoking powder and fire erupted in the courtyard;
> between endless mountains and the plain, horse hooves
> came out of the north, and there was murder and wailing
> and whirling flags and banners encircling me like magic clouds,
> like the patched clothes of refugees.
> I saw the torrential Yellow River
> by moonlight unfolding into a silver white elegy
> keening for history and silence.
> Where are the familiar streets, people and sounds?
> And where are the seven-leaved tree and new grass,
> the river's song beneath a bridge
>   of my dreams?
> There is only the blood of an old man selling flowers
>   clotting my soul,
> only the burned houses, the rubble and ruins
> gradually sinking into shifting sands
> and turning into dreams, into a wasteland.

In this myth of China the end of history is the end of beauty, and China ends up "a wasteland." In another poem in the series, however, the poet gives himself the power to redeem this "decrepit century":

> . . . because of me an eerie light will permeate these ruins
> and I'll hear music from this wasteland of stones.
>
>   *from* "An Elegy for Poetry"

The poet nurses from nature, "from swollen buds like breasts," and discovers a "renewed dignity and a holy love." Here the poet is not so much the representative victim as a lover whose holy love will refertilize the wasteland, or a shaman whose natural powers can ritually purify the broken land:

> As a poet
> when I want the rose to bloom, it will blossom;

freedom will come back carrying a small shell
where you can hear echoes of a howling storm.
Daybreak will return, the key of dawn will unlock
the wailing forests, and ripe fruits will shoot out flame.
I too will return, exhume my suffering again,
and begin to plough this land drifted in snow.

from "An Elegy for Poetry"

In this and other poems Yang Lian echoes the persistent mythos of so much of Western Modernism (Eliot's *The Waste Land*, Pound's "Canto XLVII," and Williams's *Kora in Hell* are the obvious examples, though even such texts as Nathanael West's *Miss Lonelyhearts* and Dashiell Hammett's *Red Harvest* incorporate it) in which the cycling of the seasons and of agriculture is conflated with a cycle of sex and death and with the recurrent myth of the dead god's rebirth to fertilize the dead land. In his poem "Sowing" he even volunteers himself to be the sacrificed god, with a faith in the recuperative powers of a shattered culture that sometimes eluded his Western counterparts in that earlier "lost generation."

Of all his counterparts, his mythification of the process of cultural renewal in "Sowing" seems most in keeping with the Williams of *Spring and All* who is happy to shout out "THE WORLD IS NEW." In *Spring and All* "the artist figure of / the farmer—composing / —antagonist" is a figure for the poet ("in his head / the harvest already planted"). In the title poem, spring comes to the dead land "on the road to the contagious hospital," quickening the soil but also the people, who "enter the new world naked" like Adam and Eve and, plantlike, are rooted in the earth:

—Still the profound change
has come upon them: rooted, they
grip down and begin to awaken.

The awakening of culture, then, occurs when the harvest planted by the artist comes to life. In "Sowing," Yang Lian has a dream in which he "dreamt [he] was a shuddering field of wheat, / ripe, swaying like thousands of suns," and, desiring that this harvest time come back to China and resuscitate its cultural wasteland, he asks to become the ritual sacrifice:

Bury me deep in the warm earth
and let my blood flow into underground rivers
to water shriveled hearts
from the miserable past.
I am a seed where life has hibernated,
a green fire burning vitally;

> I will raise my sprout-like hands
> into the light, reaching for sun

This theme of ritual sacrifice and renewal is perhaps the most important common element among these poets and is central to their sense of Chinese politics after Mao. They all grapple with it, though the most pessimistic among them, Mang Ke and Fei Ye, come to reject it in the end, and Gu Cheng, in his poem "Discovery" (part of his wacky and surreal series of poems about the trickster Bulin), makes a burlesque of it. In Shu Ting's poetry we see it in its most innocent form. In "Falling Leaves" she becomes "a fallen leaf, / in darkness and mud . . . wait[ing] for a soft green dream / to take its first breath from my body."

In comparison, "The Burial of the Dead" section of Eliot's *The Waste Land*, in which the "Unreal City" of London is a city of the dead, of channeled crowds presided over by the clocktower at Saint Mary Woolnoth, shows the same ritual as an ironic and grotesque gesture, rendered in hyperbolic language; any notion that the writing or reading of poetry retains the incantatory power to nurture life in the wasteland is decisively undermined in the last line of this section by Eliot's echo of Baudelaire's confrontation/identification with the hypocritical reader:

> There I saw one I knew, and stopped him, crying: "Stetson!
> "You who were with me in the ships at Mylae!
> "That corpse you planted last year in your garden,
> "Has it begun to sprout? Will it bloom this year?
> "Or has the sudden frost disturbed its bed?
> "O keep the Dog far hence, that's friend to men,
> "Or with his nails he'll dig it up again!
> "You! hypocrite lecteur!—mon semblable,—mon frère!"

But it would be wrong to assert that Yang Lian's poetry is always in Williams's camp. In some of his poems he has full measure of Eliot's world-weary cynicism, particularly in his "Nuorilang" series of poems. The Western poets drew on Christ, Osiris, Kora/Persephone, Adonis, Tamuz, and the Parsifal myth to revitalize poetry; Yang Lian seems to have drawn both on the Western tradition and on his own engagement with Tibetan gods and ceremony, which he turns into a fierce, bloody, primitive poetry in the "Nuorilang" poems, titled after the Tibetan god of virility.

To understand the Nuorilang series it is important to avoid reading it narrowly as a nonironic representation of Tibetan myth; it is also a subtle analogue for Chinese politics. Certain poems in the series carry a strong political weight when we consider that Mao, as we have seen in the poetry of Gu Cheng and Mang Ke, is strongly associated with the sun, a blood-thirsty sun that in Yang Lian's poem "Sun Tide" "waits with a mad appetite for doom to fall." At this point a poem like "His Blood Ceremony," which describes ritual sacrifices ostensibly to the god Nuorilang (but also to "the sun"), begins to take on the bloody overtones of the Cultural Revolution.

Early in the Cultural Revolution a cult of Mao developed in which Mao, referred to as the "Son of Heaven," began to wrap himself in the colors, symbols, and godlike status of the Chinese emperors. In China, after the film *The Last Emperor* came out, it was common wisdom that director Bertolucci had it wrong: Pu Yi was not the last emperor—Mao was. Yang Lian is of a generation old enough to have directly experienced this cult of Mao in which young people participated in ecstatic dances to Mao, and in which it was common to worship before his photograph on a household altar, making promises of revolutionary achievement in the morning, and confessing their failures at night. With this reading, the portrayal in "His Blood Ceremony" of an egotistical god who asks his worshippers to "Feed me with the blood of slaughtered babies and your cut-open hands so I can live forever" becomes a condemnation of the worship of this charismatic revolutionary leader which led to so much violence.

"A hot seduction comes from the abyss," says Nuorilang, "and I fill it with waves and storm." In these poems he is a vision of potent man-hood, proud, full of braggadacio, demanding sex with water nymphs in one moment, and in the next demanding human sacrifices from his male worshippers: in "Final Drum" he proclaims, "My light will illuminate you, though your life flares out like a meteor." Certainly we are presented with a myth of renewal here, but when Nuorilang exults that "the world has begun!" we know that the newborn world has been anointed in blood and is presided over by a megalomaniac. Nuorilang, the god of virility, smiling like the portrait of Mao over the Gate of Heavenly Peace in Tiananmen Square, wants others to make him immortal with their sacrifice; he is the inversion of—the dark counterpart of—the poet, who wants to make the land live again by planting the vital seed of his own body.

In Mang Ke's "Ape Herd" we see a similar attempt to blend recent Chinese history with an ironized wasteland myth. In the "Prologue" Mang Ke sketches a mythic creation in which the "ape herd" from which humanity evolves originates out of cosmic incest between brother sun and sister earth. Like the heavenly bodies, humanity engages in a series of Promethean encounters, channeling the rivers, discovering tool use, and finally "steal[ing] seeds of fire from the sun." The second section, an extended exploration of sexuality, conflates a grotesque human copulation with the cycles of politics and of agriculture. Its ironic refrain, "it's a good harvest this year," evokes a vegetation myth as satirically undermined as in Eliot's "Burial of the Dead":

> it's a good harvest this year
> so many corpses are buried in the earth
> that the fattened crops have a human taste
> and our kids herding on the plain
> play and eat as greedily
> as calves munching on sweet roots of grass   *from* "Ape Herd"

As the men "sow their lust" into the earth fertilized with human corpses we come to understand that this presages a red harvest, in which death holds the scythe.

The figure of the sun, the life-giver, also has the power to take lives. In this mythos he is the son of heaven, an epithet also used to describe Mao and the Chinese emperors, but it wasn't an ideal familial relationship. Punished by his father, he wants to abuse his children in turn: "the oven stoker seems hellbent on boiling / us and the carcass [of the earth] into one last stew." The nature of that stew comes clear in one extraordinary verse-paragraph, which I quote at length, where Mang Ke sketches out a Cultural Revolution landscape with a grotesquery so powerful it can only be compared to Goya's "Horrors of War" or Blake's illustrations to Dante's *Inferno*:

> it's a good harvest this year
> the sunlight could blacken over
> and the flayed skin of daylight
> let the days one by one seep to the ground
> you could find you are the offspring of monsters
> in the lamplight your body
> casting the shadow of a runt
> a man's head could blow to bits in the crowd
> dong dong dong
> strikes the bell that is a naked body
> two legs could be made to crawl like a tortoise
> and humans to learn to see with the eyes of dogs
> mouths turning into trumpets
> arseholes blaring non-stop talk
>   the brightest stars drown in the flood
>   while sons of bitches rule the sky
> there is love between the stones
> while bones are locked in rapt embrace
> the faces of the living blow with flies
> while rats dare their utmost in the struggle against us

> humanity rotten to the core
> people nail their own coffins
> slander gallops, rumour moves crabwise
> carnivores peck their meat,
> in the cavities of empty heads
> the spider spins at leisure
> and one healthy chap
> drowns in his own piss
> the dead continue their quarrels underground
> in heaven the gods are red in tooth and claw
> the sun disappears for the distant mountains
> like a wounded tiger on the run who stains
> his blood across the last of twilight
> after disaster
> so many are skin and bone
> that a gust of wind is enough
> to blow them away   *from* "Ape Herd"

We see at last that the genesis that Mang Ke is describing is a genesis of death, a creation myth in which the world, created from incest and violence, becomes a wasteland, a "dead expanse of land" populated by human monsters who echo the domestic violence of the gods on a national level. Is it a surprise then that Mang Ke concludes that the only comfort is that after such horror "death will be / a sensation perhaps to be savoured"? "Ape Herd" is an unrelenting vision of humanity's degeneracy and evil. Evolution, the myth of progress, historical determinacy, myths of renewal, all these are conflated, and all of them undermined—evolution turned to devolution, progress turned to regress, history become the cycles of hell, and renewal become the renewed atrocities of each generation. Mang Ke entertains no illusions about the grand role of the poet in this hellish litany; we do not see, as in Yang Lian, Bei Dao, and Shu Ting, a presentation of the poet as savior, of poetic creation as an antidote to history gone awry. His pessimism is so deep that even the language in which he writes is reduced in the last lines of the poem to a bestial wail:

> across the wilderness there echo
> the plaintive sounds of our crying
> as if bequeathed from remotest history
> the tragic gibber of the ape herd.   *from* "Ape Herd"

I'd like to end this discussion with a number of younger poets, many of them still in their formative years, whom I believe deserve to be discovered. They are of the generation immediately following that of the Misty poets, and range from Bei Ling's position as a younger admirer, friend, and imitator to the openly hostile position of Wang Xiaoling, who, as Michelle Yeh notes, splits with the Misties because of their overreliance on image-centered poetry.[33]

Consider the complicated case of a poet like Fei Ye. Tall and sardonic, from the cold northern province of *Heilongjian* (Black Dragon River), he is younger than the Misties and considers himself outside of their school. Perhaps the fact that they have begun to receive press in the West as well as China has already made them such a threat to his generation of poets that he must break with them and stake out his own territory. He has strong affinities with the dark vision of Baudelaire, especially with Baudelaire's aggressions against the reader, which he weds with the difficult, often obscure, dissident politics of Mandelstam, whose work Fei Ye has translated into Chinese. He also has a special love for Kafka's absurdist nightmares and keeps a portrait of him on his livingroom wall, and at the same time he considers Whitman as much a model as the other three. No surprise then that his poems are filled with sperm, violence, and bitter political invective. The Transcendentalists' strongest mark on him is perhaps that in the cause of self-reliance he will acknowledge influences one day that he will bitterly denounce the next. A sampling of lines from "The Curse" shows that his bitterness derives from an acute awareness of the politics of totalitarianism:

> Hit men and victims depend on each other
> And there is no road to the past, never has been.
>
> Silence, the greatest weapon, has been brought to bear:
> No words, no songs, no crying.
>
> As stars pursue their ancient games
> . . . the people wait for death and gape like fish.

Yet he has the balance of judgment to understand the inequities of the capitalist system as well. "America," he says, "I can't see you. / I will never get out of your ghettos." America may be "like science fiction" but he doesn't sing her praises like Walt Whitman:

> Whitman you old schemer,
> The TV antennas have snipped your great beard.
> Your sons and grandsons
> Have only the pain of poverty.
> Murder, suicide, nothing is new in America
>   of which you sang.
>
> *from* "The Poet in America"

One of the most exciting recent developments in Chinese poetry is that—after a first generation of poets in which Shu Ting was the only major female talent—a group of young, direct, confessional women poets has succeeded her, continuing her task of exploring the suppressed emotional center of the nation, but broadening the scope of the discussion. In Tang Yaping's intensely sexual suite "Black Desert," she assembles a darkly readable set of sexual symbols—the black swamp, stalactites in the black cave, the clitoral vortex, the orgasm of sudden rain—and deals directly with masturbation and the blind ecstacy of orgasm:

> . . . my hair strays wildly with desire
>   and I am ravished by night
> This desire is an endless darkness
> I keep stroking the darkest spot for a long time
> watching as it turns to a black vortex
> powerful enough to seduce the sun and moon   *from* "Black Swamp"

> In a glorious moment women disappear in a blind world
>
>   *from* "Black Cave"

In "Black Gold" she dramatizes the frustrations of a sexually active woman in a sexist society:

> The problem with me is the problem with gold
> —everyone plunders me
>   then hoards me with all the love there is
> Each night is a chasm
> All of you possess me
>   only the way night holds fireflies
> Listen. My soul will turn into misty smoke
> to make my corpse docile and obedient   *from* "Black Gold"

Like Tang Yaping, Zhang Zhen discovers her sexuality with abandon; in her masturbation poem "New Discovery," the discovery she makes "between the bedroom and living room" is that of her own femaleness. Her poem "A Desire" reinvents the elegiac poem of lost love that is so familiar in Shu Ting, charging the tired genre with sensual excitement:

> He begins by kissing my neck
> then smears burning liquor all over my body
> His hair stands up like noon sunlight
> I am begging
> but he climbs over the mountains where my soul lives
> and then drifts away
> Only the double oars we have used are left
> in the reeds corroding   *from* "A Desire"

Conversely, the guilt and rage of her poem "Abortion" matches anything in Sylvia Plath or Anne Sexton:

> For this imagined relationship
> mother and son
> you and me
> I've already sharpened the knife
> Blood fireworks up in glorious patterns onto the ceiling
> A pair of skinny legs upside down

There is no expressing the intense courage and innovation this represents for a Chinese woman poet of the new generation.

There are also important new talents in the new generation of male poets: the delightful, romantic lyrics of Xi Chuan often paint pictures of horses, like a Chinese James Wright, while the surreal half-narratives that form the poetry of his friend Bei Ling defy classification—they create moments of lucid insanity, sketch out interior landscapes, veer in and out of symbolism, as if he were a kind of apprentice Tomas Tranströmer. Ha Jin is a poet who works in English and lives now in America, yet, as he writes me in a letter, "without question, I am a Chinese writer, not an American-Chinese poet, though I write in English. If this sounds absurd, the absurdity is historical rather than personal . . . since I can hardly publish anything in Chinese now." His first book, *Between Silences*, chronicles the '60s and '70s in China in first-person confessional poems and in dramatic monologues. He wrote it in English because "after June 1989 I realized that I could not return to China in the near future if I wanted to be a writer who has the freedom to write." Modern Chinese literature, that troubled thing, has been able to speak only between long periods of silence. In his poem, "Because I Will Be Silenced" Ha Jin states the necessity of writing poems that "strive to break the walls/that cut off people's voices":

> But I will be silenced.
> The starred tie around my neck
> at any moment can tighten into a cobra.
>
> How can I speak about coffee and flowers?
>
> *from* "Because I Will Be Silenced"

One of the best of the younger poets is Chou Ping, whose witty, lyrical absurdity (so different from the almost Dada buffoonery of Gu Cheng's recent poems) is a fresh voice in a generation that has so much to say of violence and despair. Like Ha Jin he writes in English, a habit he caught while studying creative writing with Willis Barnstone at the Beijing Foreign Studies University. The majority of these poems were written before he had ever left China, though "9 Flights Between 2 Continents" deals with his transition from teacher in China to graduate student at Indiana University. His "Ways of Looking at a Poet," a bow in the direction of

Wallace Stevens's "Thirteen Ways of Looking at a Blackbird," suggests varying roles for the new Chinese poet: humble, surviving a hostile world by flexibility ("an admirable punching sack, receiving / every blow with an appreciative bow"); rebellious and angry ("a rage enclosed in a free balloon"); or, more traditionally, as pure medium, as a Buddhist absence facing the world ("a broken mirror / with godlike indifference / sleeping open-eyed"). It is perhaps the best mark of the poet that Chou Ping can play all these roles with equal facility.

In another early poem he expresses his debt to Whitman—"you took me in your hand / like picking up a snail shell / or the scroll of a broken violin / and uncoiled me into a river / whorled and fingerprinted with a mysterious force in the dark, / O Walt Whitman!" It is, however, in his long poem "A Journey to Babel" that we first see him taking on the Whitmanian role of poet-prophet. Here, in place of absolute truths, he attempts to create something like Stevens's mutable dream of poetry as a redemptive Supreme Fiction or to stand as Whitman's representative man in a society where language is tossed down and where the role allocated to the poet is exile:

> but you are now
> a solid dream in my hand
> —the cooled ruins
> of the Tower of Babel.
>
> O stars,
> storm-tossed bricks
> of the stillborn tower,
> exiled poets
> from Plato's Eden—
> stop yelling
>   with your twisting bodies
>   in darkness and birthpang,
> come down
>   in a meteor shower
> and build a tower
>   in each heart—
> Should silence be
>   the universal language
>   if man recognizes
> the inner light
>   is
>   One?   *from* "A Journey to Babel"

Chou Ping is the least political of these poets; his values are human values, not dogmatic ones, and he is foremost a gentle idealist, a bemused spectator of a confused world. As such, after the poetics of nightmare we have seen in Bei Dao, Jiang He, Duo Duo, Gu Cheng, and Fei Ye, in the ruins of Tiananmen Square as the Chinese authorities clean up through a process of systematic repression of dissidence, and through the straight-faced denial and distortion of history that Orwell first predicted, Chou Ping is a good note on which to end this discussion. There is some comfort in believing that the world can be transformed by poetry, that "silence" will not "be / the universal language," and that there is something in us that makes us sing in the cage like Lear and Cordelia as "God's Spies" and "wear out, in a wall'd prison, packs and sects of great ones, that ebb and flow by the moon."

NOTES

1. See the discussions in Mosher, Steven W., *China Misperceived: American Illusions and Chinese Reality*, Basic Books, New York, 1990, pp. 35–39, and in Fairbank, John King, *The United States and China*, 4th ed., Harvard University Press, Cambridge, Mass., 1980, pp. 155–58.

2. The term Misty (*menglong*) was originally a term of derision applied to the new generation of poets by their old-school Social Realist critics. It was meant to refer insultingly to the elusive quality of the new poetry, but the Misty poets reversed the intent of the term and took it on as a badge of pride.

3. "Hairdressers Do It In Style," *China Daily*, 15 Sept. 1984, p. 3.

4. He Li, "The Discussion Concerning the Question of Western Modernism and the Direction of the Development of Chinese Literature, Being Held in *Literary Gazette (Wenyibao)* and Other Journals and Papers," in *Trees on the Mountain: An Anthology of New Chinese Writing*, eds. Stephen C. Soong and John Minford, Chinese University Press, Hong Kong, 1984, p. 53.

5. Mao Zedong, "Talks at the Yenan Forum on Literature," in *Modern Literature from China*, eds. Walter J. Meserve and Ruth L. Meserve, New York University Press, New York, 1974, p. 297.

6. Mao, ibid., p. 302.

7. Mao, ibid., p. 298.

8. Mao, ibid., pp. 308–309.

9. Mao, ibid., p. 301.

10. He, op cit., p. 50.

11. He, op cit., p. 50.

12. He, op cit., p. 51.

13. The name echoes a "Democratic Wall" in Beijing University where students criticized the Communist Party in an earlier period of free debate about literature and society, the Hundred Flowers Campaign of 1956–1957.

14. "Call for Writers to Be Guaranteed Literary Freedom," *China Daily*, Vol. 4 (1071), 31 Dec. 1984, p. 1.

15. "Criticism Ad," Editorial, *China Daily*, 19 June 1985, p. 4. Reprinted from the *Worker's Daily*.

16. Xu Jingya, "Keeping the Socialist Orientation of Literature and Art Constantly in Mind," in *Trees on the Mountain: An Anthology of New Chinese Writing*, eds. Stephen C. Soong and John Minford, Chinese University Press, Hong Kong, 1984, p. 68.

17. Lamarche, Gara, "Writing is a Dangerous Occupation in Much of the World," *Poets and Writers*, Vol. 18 (6), Nov./Dec. 1990, p. 46.

18. Spence, Jonathan D., *The Search for Modern China*, W. W. Norton, New York, 1990, p. 719 ff.

19. *Chinese Literature* No. 8, Beijing: Foreign Language Press, 1966, p. 98.

20. Lin, Julia C., *Modern Chinese Poetry: An Introduction*, University of Washington Press, Seattle, 1972, p. 229.

21. Hong Huang, "The New Poetry—A Turning Point? (A Misty Manifesto)," translated by Zhu Zhiyu with John Minford, in *Trees on the Mountain: An Anthology of New Chinese Writing*, eds. Stephen C. Soong and John Minford, Chinese University Press, Hong Kong, 1984, pp. 53, 191.

22. Hong, ibid., p. 193.

23. Hong, ibid., p. 191.

24. Hemingway, Ernest, *A Farewell to Arms*, Charles Scribner's Sons, New York, 1929, 1959, pp. 184–85.

25. Hong, op cit., p. 192.

26. Hong, op cit., p. 193–94.

27. Hong, op cit., p. 194.

28. Yang Lian, "Tradition and Us," translated by Ginger Li, in *Trees on the Mountain: An Anthology of New Chinese Writing*, eds. Stephen C. Soong and John Minford, Chinese University Press, Hong Kong, 1984, p. 73.

29. Yang, ibid., p. 71.

30. Orwell, George, "Politics and the English Language," from *Shooting the Elephant and Other Essays*, reprinted in *20th Century Literary Criticism: A Reader*, ed. David Lodge, Longman, New York, 1972, p. 369.

31. Thoreau, Henry David, *Walden and Civil Disobedience: Authoritative Texts, Background, Reviews and Essays in Criticism*, ed. Owen Thomas, Norton, New York, 1966, pp. 64–65.

32. Spence, op cit., p. 606.

33. Yeh, Michelle, *Modern Chinese Poetry: Theory and Practice Since 1917*, Yale University Press, New Haven, Conn., 1991, p. 85.

The Misty Poets

# Bei Dao

A Day

Lock up your secrets with a drawer
leave notes in the margin of a favourite book
put a letter in the pillarbox and stand in silence a while
size up passers-by in the wind, without misgivings
study shop windows with flashing neon lights
insert a coin in the telephone room
cadge a smoke from the fisherman under the bridge
as the river steamer sounds its vast siren
stare at yourself through clouds of smoke
in the full-length dim mirror at the theatre entrance
and when the curtain has shut out the clamour of the sea
    of stars
leaf through faded photos and old letters in the lamplight.

A Country Night

Evening sunshine and distant hills
fold into a crescent moon
passing through an elm wood
the bird nest is empty
a path encircles the pond
chasing a dog with a dirty coat
up to the mud wall at the village entrance
the bucket in the well sways gently

the clock is as still
as the roller in the yard
dried wheat stalks stir uneasily
the sound of chewing from the stable
is full of threat
a man's long shadow
slips down the doorstep
firelight from a kitchen range
casts a ruddy glow on a woman's arms
and a chipped earthenware bowl

Night: Theme and Variations

Here the roads converge
parallel beams of light
are a longwinded but abruptly interrupted dialogue
suffused with the drivers' pungent smoke
and rough muttered curses
railings have replaced the queues
the lamplight seeping out from between cracks in the
    doorboards
is cast with the cigarette butts onto the roadside
for nimble feet to tread on
an old man's forgotten walking stick against a billboard
looks as if it were ready to go
the stone waterlily has withered
in the fountain tall buildings slowly topple
the rising moon suddenly strikes
the hour again and again
arousing ancient Time inside the palace wall
the sundial calibrates errors as it turns
waiting for the grand rite of the dawn
brocade dress ribbons stand up rustling in the wind
brushing away the dust from the stone steps
the shadow of a tramp slinks past the wall
red and green neon lights blaze for him
and keep him from sleeping all night

a lost cat scurries up a bench
gazing down at the smoke-soft gleam of the waves
but the mercury vapour lamp rudely opening the curtain
to peer at the secrets that others store
disturbs the dream wakens the lonely
behind a small door
a hand gently draws the catch
as if pulling a rifle bolt

In a Decade

Over the forgotten land
the years entangled with the horse's yoke bells
rang throughout the night, and the road's panting
under the swaying load changed into a song
passed on by people everywhere
to the sound of an incantation a woman's necklace
rose into the night sky as if in affirmation
the fluorescent dial struck licentiously at will
time is as honest as a wrought-iron fence
except for the wind trimmed by withered branches
no one can pass over it or come and go
flowers that have only bloomed in books
eternally imprisoned become the mistress of truth
but yesterday's broken lamp
is so resplendent in the hearts of the blind
right up until the time when they are shot
a final portrait of the assassin is left behind
in eyes that have suddenly opened

The Oranges Are Ripe

The oranges are ripe,
Dripping with sun, the oranges
are ready.

Let me
walk into your heart,
heavy with love.

The oranges are ripe.
The rind sprays
a delicate mist.
                    Let me
walk into your heart,
my grief dissolving
into blissful tears.

The oranges are ripe.
Bitter threads web every
sun-drenched segment.
                    Let me
walk into your heart to gather
my dismembered dream.

The oranges are ripe,
dripping with sun. The oranges
are ready.

Declaration

for Yu Luoke

Perhaps the final hour is come
I have left no testament
Only a pen, for my mother
I am no hero
In an age without heroes
I just want to be a man

The still horizon
Divides the ranks of the living and the dead
I can only choose the sky

I will not kneel on the ground
Allowing the executioners to look tall
The better to obstruct the wind of freedom

From star-like bullet holes shall flow
A blood-red dawn.

Answer

The scoundrel carries his baseness around like an ID card.
The honest man bears his honor like an epitaph.
Look—the gilded sky is swimming
with undulant reflections of the dead.

They say the ice age ended years ago.
Why are there icicles everywhere?
The Cape of Good Hope has already been found.
Why should all those sails contend on the Dead Sea?

I came into this world with nothing
but paper, rope, and shadow.
Now I come to be judged,
and I've nothing to say but this:

Listen. *I don't believe!*
OK. You've trampled
a thousand enemies underfoot. Call me
a thousand and one.

I don't believe the sky is blue.
I don't believe what the thunder says.
I don't believe dreams aren't real,
that beyond death there is no reprisal.

If the sea should break through the sea-wall,
let its brackish water fill my heart.
If the land should rise from the sea again,

we'll choose again to live in the heights.

The earth revolves. A glittering constellation
pricks the vast defenseless sky.
Can you see it there? that ancient ideogram—
the eye of the future, gazing back.

Nightmare

On the shifting wind
I painted an eye
then the blocked moment passed
but no one awoke
the nightmare still overflowed in the sunshine
spilling across the river bed, creeping over the cobbles
provoking new friction and strife
in the branches, on the eaves
the birds' frightened gazes froze into ice
and dropped to earth
then a thin layer of frost
formed over the ruts in the road
no one awoke

The Old Temple

Fading chimes
form cobwebs
       spreading annual rings
in splintered columns
without memories
     a stone
spreads an echo through the misty valley
a stone
       without memories
when a small path wound its way here

the dragons and strange birds flew away
carrying off the mute bells under the eaves
once a year indifferently
weeds grow not caring
whether the master they submit to is
a monk's cloth shoe
   or wind
the stele is chipped, the inscription worn away
as if only in a general conflagration
could it be deciphered
   yet perhaps
with a glance from the living
the tortoise might come back to life in the earth
and crawl over the threshold
   bearing its heavy secret

Coming Home at Night

After braving the music of the air raid alarm
I hang my shadow on the hat-stand
take off the dog's eyes
(which I use for escape)
remove my false teeth (these final words)
and close my astute and experienced pocket watch
(that garrisoned heart)

The hours fall in the water one after the other
in my dreams like depth bombs
they explode

The Morning's Story

A word has abolished another word
a book has issued orders
to burn another book

a morning established by the violence of language
has changed the morning
of people's coughing

Maggots attack the kernel
the kernel comes from dull valleys
from among dull crowds
the government finds its spokesman
cats and mice
have similar expressions

On the road in the sky
the armed forester examines
the sun which rumbles past
over the asphalt lake
he hears the sound of disaster
the untrammeled sound of a great conflagration

Requiem

for the victims of June Fourth

Not the living but the dead
under the doomsday-purple sky
go in groups
suffering guides forward suffering
at the end of hatred is hatred
the spring has run dry, the conflagration stretches unbroken
the road back is even further away

Not gods but the children
amid the clashing helmets
say their prayers
mothers breed light
darkness breeds mothers
the stone rolls, the clock runs backwards
the eclipse of the sun has taken place

Not your bodies but your souls
shall share a common birthday every year
You are all the same age
love has founded for the dead
an everlasting alliance
you embrace each other closely
in the massive register of deaths

Beyond

A tempest in a teacup leads the marching sea.
Beyond the harbor, adrift on their sleepless bed,
the coupling lovers make fast the chains of power.
Beyond the frame, a plaster figure wearing a classical smile
speaks from the manifold shadows of one day.
Beyond credulity, a race horse outruns death.
Implacably, the moon imprints its seal upon black happenings.
Beyond the story, a plastic tree is thrashing in the wind.
This dismal fare is our excuse for survival.

Midnight Singer

A song
is a thief who flees across rooftops
making off with the rest of the spectrum,
having set the red hour-hand
on four o'clock, kingdom come.
When four o'clock explodes
in the rooster's head,
it's four o'clock madness.

A song
is an implacably rancorous tree
across the border,

loosing promise after promise,
a pack of wolves that will devour the future.

A song
is a mirror that remembers your body,
an emperor of memory,
a flame
that wax tongues speak,
a flower suckled by myth,
a steam locomotive
hurtling into a church.

A song
is the death of the singer,
the night of his death
pressed on a coal-black record,
sung over and over and over.

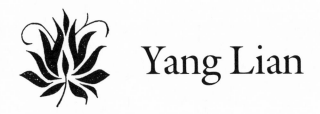

Yang Lian

from the poem cycle "Bell on the Frozen Lake"

An Ancient Children's Tale

How should I savor these bright memories,
their glowing gold, shining jade, their tender radiance like silk
that washed over me at birth?
All around me were industrious hands, flourishing peonies,
    and elegant upturned eaves.
Banners, inscriptions, and the names of nobility were everywhere,
and so many temple halls where bright bells sang into my ears.
Then my shadow slipped over the fields and mountains, rivers
    and springtime
as all around my ancestors' cottages I sowed
towns and villages like stars of jade and gemstones.
Flames from the fire painted my face red; plowshares and pots
clattered out their bright music and poetry
which wove into the sky during festivals.
How should I savor these bright memories?
When I was young I gazed down at the world,
watching purple grapes, like the night, drift in from the west
and spill over in a busy street. Every drop of juice became a star
set into the bronze mirror where my glowing face looked back.
My heart blossomed like the earth or the ocean at daybreak
as camel bells and sails painted like frescos embarked
from where I was to faraway lands to clink the gold coin
    of the sun.

When I was born
I would laugh even at
the glazed and opulent palaces, at the bloody red
walls, and at the people rapt in luxurious dreams
for centuries in their incense-filled chambers.
I sang my pure song to them with passion,
but never stopped to think
why pearls and beads of sweat drain to the same place,
these rich tombs filled with emptiness,
or why in a trembling evening
a village girl should wander down to the river,
her eyes so clear and bright with grief.

In the end, smoking powder and fire erupted in the courtyard;
between endless mountains and the plain, horse hooves
came out of the north, and there was murder and wailing
and whirling flags and banners encircling me like magic clouds,
like the patched clothes of refugees.
I saw the torrential Yellow River
by moonlight unfolding into a silver white elegy
keening for history and silence.
Where are the familiar streets, people and sounds?
And where are the seven-leaved tree and new grass,
the river's song beneath a bridge
        of my dreams?
There is only the blood of an old man selling flowers
        clotting my soul,
only the burned houses, the rubble and ruins
gradually sinking into shifting sands
and turning into dreams, into a wasteland.

An Elegy for Poetry

The decrepit century's bony brow protrudes
and its wounded shoulders shiver.
Snow buries the ruins—below this whiteness an undertow
of uneasiness, through the deep shadows of trees it drifts,
and a stray voice is broadcast across time.

There is no way
through this land which death has made an enigma.

The decrepit century deceives its children,
leaving unreadable calligraphy and snow
on the stones everywhere to augment the ornamental decay.
My hands cling to a sheaf of my poems.
When my unnamed moment arrives, call me!
But the wind's small skiff scuds off bearing history
and on my heels like a shadow
an ending follows.

Now I understand it all.
To sob out loud refutes nothing when the fingers of young girls
and the shy myrtle are drowned in purple thorn brush.
From the eyes meteors streak into the endless sea
but I know that in the end all souls will rise again,
soaked with the fresh breath of the sea,
with eternal smiles, with voices that refuse humiliation,
and climb into blue heaven.
There I can read out my poems.

I will believe every icicle is a sun,
that because of me an eerie light will permeate these ruins
and I'll hear music from this wasteland of stones.
I'll suckle from swollen buds like breasts
and have renewed dignity and a holy love.
I'll bare my heart in these clean white snowfields
as I do in the clean white sky
and as a poet
challenge this decrepit century.

As a poet
when I want the rose to bloom, it will blossom;
freedom will come back carrying a small shell
where you can hear echoes of a howling storm.
Daybreak will return, the key of dawn will unlock
the wailing forests, and ripe fruits will shoot out flame.
I too will return, exhume my suffering again,
and begin to plough this land drifted in snow.

Sowing

I dreamt I was a shuddering field of wheat,
ripe, swaying like thousands of suns,
and even the hot winds were golden,
calmly singing me
a delicate song
soft as an ancient smile,
like a blurred blessing from afar.

Let my desires spill over
and my love be sown.

Bury me deep in the warm earth
and let my blood flow into underground rivers
to water shriveled hearts
from the miserable past.
I am a seed where life has hibernated,
a green fire burning vitally;
I will raise my sprout-like hands
into the light, reaching for sun
and from the earth suck out courage and force
enough to beat down death and this harsh fate.

Let my desires spill over
and my love be sown.

I am proud to be close to the earth;
even when winter stars are frozen over or under snowdrifts
I think of the coming hope of spring
and of the next sure harvest;
after growing pains
I now know that joy is in faith,
and my only duty is to create abundance.
Storms may have whipped me in the past and may again
but I'll watch as my children laugh
and run after new dreams,
and my wounds will heal
as the songs of harvest drift up over the villages.

Let my desires spill over
and my love be sown.

from the poem cycle "Nuorilang"[1]

Solar Tide

The high plateau like a violent tiger is burning brightly on the shore of
the angry tide.
O, light is everything, a round setting sun floods toward you and the
earth hangs in air.

Pirate sails billow into arms, rocks spread for breasts, and hawks tear at
a heart.[2]
A shepherd's solitude is swallowed up in endless tremulous
thickets.
Prayer flags, symbols of a screaming faith, drift over the pure
blue.

Now what lost white scarf of cloud will you grieve for,
enduring the ondriven dusk, here under time's heel.
On the desert horizon thousands of tombstones are anchored like
castaway plows.
Forsaking each other, they are forsaken forever: let copper return to the
earth and let blood turn to rust.
Will you still weep with every storm?
The western wind perpetually awakens a goldminer's fortune in the
deep sands.
The log path along the cliff edge has collapsed, no way to pass, and the
shadowed caves are black,
but the sky of ancient sorceresses once again reveals the myth of the
seven lotuses.

O light, holy glaze, worshiping fire and dancing with fire,
you bathe away the murmured pain, and give the sky the peace of a
broken clay pot.

Did this tremendous instant shake you up?
The sun still waits with a mad appetite for doom to fall.

1. Nuorilang, a Tibetan word meaning "male god," is the Tibetan god of virility.

2. In the Tibetan "sky burial" the dead are skinned, chopped up, their bones crushed and mixed with the flesh, and then left on a rock for the hawks, eagles, kites, and buzzards to eat.

Nuorilang, the Golden Tree

I am the god of waterfalls and of snow mountains,
I am huge, potent, the new moon appears when I dictate,
and only I am ruler of the rivers.
All kinds of birds inhabit my chest,
a tangled forest shadows the trail to the secret pool.
I am bold as a flight of young stags
and my desire is the month of March when forces of unrest gather.

I am the golden tree,
a tree nourished with gold.
A hot seduction comes from the abyss
and I fill it with waves and storm,
ignoring the proverbs of cowards who surround me.

Wandering women, your reflections bright in the water,
who among you will tempt me to drink?

My eyes conquer the night
as twelve long horns rein in the wild pomegranate winds.
Wherever I am, shadows are gone
and with my touch each strawberry becomes a flaming star shooting
     from the universe's core.
I am a real man. I possess you all.

His Blood Ceremony

Surround white skulls with a map of dark red to worship sun and war;
Feed me with the blood of slaughtered babies and your cut-open hands
     so I can live forever.

An obsidian knife slices open the earth's chest cavity, the heart is handed
     high in the air
as countless flags, like warrior drums, flap into the sunset.
I am alive, smiling, proud to lead you to conquer death;
use my blood as a signature on history, to decorate this wasteland, this
     ceremony.

Now, let your grief wash away! Let the monster cliff block the challenge
     of mountain ranges
and battering eagles dash in to peck the eyes until only empty sockets
     are left.
Let bodies twisted or in repose on the sacrificial altar burst all at once
     into fierce bloom.
Now lost hope comes back astride dread hungers, leaving a wake of sonic
     booms and praises.
What made you find this solitary glory on the horizon
as your body's blood drains away? Going willingly to death is greater
     glory than death itself.

Be devout to me! Then forty virgins will sing in praise of you,
their dark and candid skin like bronze bells, they'll fast in anticipation
     and promenade
with a noble, abject, pure, sinful, immaculate, filthy tide,
as my vast memory, my secret, is gradually born in the shuddering ritual.
A pagoda gorgeously erect shows the road to heaven for twilight on the
     mountain peaks;
you are released from this pool of blood to approach the gods.

Final Drum

Now the high plateau, a violent tiger, is endlessly caressed by transparent
   fingers.
Now the disordered forest, shining and stern, stretches out its trampled
   beauty,
revealing the harmony of the universe to mountain floods and the piled
   cairns of destroyed villages.
Tree roots stubbornly stride like gigantic human feet, children smile as
   they wander,
dignity and self are reincarnated, and the lilies of the valley sing out my
   holiness.
My light will illuminate you, though your life flares out like a meteor;
its golden call gave the ocean its sorrow, making it restless forever.
Through dark nights, oblivion, whispered dreams and a distant
   summons,
right now, from the world's core I say, my people, let us live.
The world has begun! Birds are singing. Everything is enlightenment.

Shu Ting

Perhaps

—reply to the loneliness of a poet

Perhaps our hearts
    will have no reader
Perhaps we took the wrong road
    and so we end up lost

Perhaps we light one lantern after another
    storms blow them out one by one
Perhaps we burn our life-candle against the dark
    but no fire warms the body

Perhaps once we're out of tears
    the land will be fertilized
Perhaps while we praise the sun
    we are also sung by the sun

Perhaps the heavier the monkey on our shoulders
    the more we believe
Perhaps we can only protest others' suffering
    silent to our own misfortune
Perhaps
    because this call is irresistable
        we have no other choice

December, 1979

Assembly Line

Night after night,
the assembly line of time.
After work at the factory's assembly line
we join the homebound lines
as stars above assemble to cross the sky.
Over there
a line of lost saplings.

Stars must be exhausted
after millenia
and no change in the itinerary
and the fullness, the color,
of the anaemic saplings
dulls in the coalsmoke.
I know this
by our shared routine.

Strangely
I cannot feel
my own existence.
Out of misery or habit I've become
like the branching trees, the assemblages of stars,
too enervated to question
this determined fate.

January–February 1980

Mother

Pale fingers brush my temples
I am a child again,
        tightly clutching a corner of your dress.
I hold on to your vanishing figure,
afraid to open my eyes
though dawn has
        scissored my dream to shreds.

I've carefully stored that bright red muffler;
washing it might take away

the slight scent of you.
Mother,
time is a cruel flow.
Memory could also be faded,
how dare I open that painted box?

When a needle pricked me, I could cry to you.
Now, I don't even sigh,
wearing a crown of thistles.
I grieve before your picture.
Even if my cry could pierce the yellow earth,
I wouldn't disturb your sleep.

I'm afraid to display these tokens of love,
though I've written many odes
to flowers, to the sea, to daybreak.
A gentle, deep yearning for you,
mother,
not cascading, not a waterfall,
but an ancient well, drowned with bushes and flowers,
singing in silence.   August 1, 1975

Missing You

A colorful hanging chart with no lines.
A pure algebra problem with no solution.
A one-string harp, stirring rosaries
that hang from dripping eaves.
A pair of oars that can never reach
the other side of the ocean.

Waiting silently like a bud.
Gazing at a distance like a setting sun.
Perhaps an ocean is hidden somewhere,
but when it flows out—only two tears.

O, in the background of a heart,
in the deep well of a soul.   1978

Encounter

My bicycle tilts like a flame tree
A bell jangle hangs in midair
Swiftly the earth backpedals
It is a night ten years past

Again my flame tree bicycle is wavering
With a fragrance of bells in the nervous street
In this ink-spreading, enveloping darkness
Your eyes burn as skylights of memory

Maybe nothing happened
Familiar roads bring illusions
But even if it did
I've grown used to this tearlessness   March 1979

Note: In the untranslatable first line, Shu Ting puns, using a tilting Phoenix tree (flame tree
in English) to describe her "Phoenix" brand bicycle, falling over.

Two or Three Incidents Recollected

An overturned cup of wine.
A stone path sailing in moonlight.
Where the blue grass is flattened,
an azalea flower abandoned.

The eucalyptus wood swirls.
Stars above teem into a kaleidoscope.
On a rusty anchor,
eyes mirror the dizzy sky.

Holding up a book to shade the candle
and with a finger in between the lips,
I sit in an eggshell quiet,
having a semi-transparent dream.

Song of a Small Window

Put down the stationery,
come to the open window.
I'm holding a lamp up high
for you—
see me from this distance.

Wind walks over the dawning earth,
sweeping the sky clean.
Night is still picking up
its broken pieces along the street.
All flowers, all green twigs
will taste another morning frost,
though crimson dawn is not far away.

The sea smell is locked behind mountains,
they can't keep on
robbing us of our youth.
And they won't delay us long.

Promise me—no tears.
Come to the window and meet me
if you feel lonely:
let's see each other's sad smile
and swap poems of struggle and joy.   1979

Dream of an Island

I'm at my own latitude
with migrant dreams—

White snow.
Ice roads.
A heavy-hanging bell
behind a red palace wall
is tearing the motionless dusk.

O, I see a cherry brook
opening its dancing skirt
after a downpour;
I see little pines
put their heads together
to make a speech;
and songs are heard in sandstorms
like a spurting fountain.

Thus, tropical suns are sparkling
under eyelashes with heavy frost;
and blood conducts
reliable spring wind
between frozen palms.
At every crossroad
blessed by streetlamps
more than love is silently promised
in the kiss goodbye.

Between sea tide and green shade
I'm having a dream against snowstorms.

Falling Leaves

I

The melting moon
was a piece of thin ice
floating on a cool canvas.
You walked me home,
giving out small sighs
all the way, though not
in disappointment or sorrow.
We never could explain the mood
leaves give us, swirling in wind,
but after the separation
I would hear your steps in falling leaves.

II

Spring is whispering to us
from all directions,
but leaves under our feet,
evidence of winter's crime,
stir up a murky memory.
Deep shocks
make our eyes avoid each other,
deeper reflections
force our thoughts to meet again.

Seasons stamp year rings in trees.
Falling and budding leaves
compose thousands of lines.
But a tree should have only
one timeless theme—
"I will never leave the earth
to spread freely into the sky."

III

Tapping my window,
wind describes your whereabouts—
you are walking under a kapok tree
and wind shakes down a rain of flowers:
spring nights are icy,
chills kept outside your heart.

Suddenly I feel: I am a fallen leaf,
in darkness and mud—
while wind plays a funeral theme
I calmly wait for a soft green dream
to take its first breath from my body.

The Gift

I dream the dream of a pond
who lives not just to mirror the sky

but to let willows trees and milk-vetch on the bank
drink me up.
I'll branch up through the roots into their veined leaves,
and when they wither I won't grieve
since I'll have articulated myself
and will have lived.

I'm happy with the joy of sunshine
whose brief life creates a masterpiece beyond time
in the pupils of children;
it will start as a tiny fire, golden,
and sing an emerald green song
among the sprouting seeds.
I am plain but abundant
which gives me depth.

When I hurt it is with the grief of migratory birds;
only the spring understands my deep love
which endures such adversity and loss
to fly toward a time of flickering warmth.
O these bloody wings
will brush out one intense line of verse
to pierce all souls and time.

Everything I feel
is a gift from the earth.

Jiang He

I. An Ancient Story

I am nailed to a prison wall.
The dark times are gathering like crows
winging in from all the world, all of history,
to peck the brave to death against this wall, one by one.
Their grief turns to stone.
They are lonelier than the mountains.
For the crime of chiseling,
of sculpting the people's character,
the heroes are nailed to death.
Wind erodes and the rain thrashes;
on the wall the blurred figures waver,
parts of arms, hands, faces are gone.
As whips lash and the beaked darkness pecks
the hands of ancestors and brothers in silent
hard labor build themselves into the wall.
I come here once again
to fight against my slave fate,
and, with my violent death, to shake the wall till it starts to crumble.
Let all the silent dead stand up and howl!

2. Suffering

My daughter is going to be shot.
The muzzle approaches me, a black sun
crossing the dry and cracked field.
Dead fingers branching from an old tree,
a face of twisted wrinkles,
this land and I suffer the same disaster.
My heart is thrown to the ground,
soil drenched with my daughter's blood.
These children's tears are also salt.
It is winter and the small rivers are freezing,
the small rivers lose their song
as the dresses of sisters, daughters and wives
are torn open, and hair flies
like surf surging on the rocks.
My hair is an ocean.
The hands of fathers, husbands, sons
toss in the hair-sea,
bone joints dully groan
like a ship,
and on the clearcut land a jungle flourishes.

4. A Date with Execution

The deceiving wind blurs windows and eyes
while the massacre takes place.
I can't hide in the house—
my blood won't let me.
The daylight of children constrains me
and I am thrown in prison.
Handcuffs and shackles burrow into my flesh,
whips and blood weave a net on my body,
my voice is sliced off,
my heart is a ball of silent fire burning my lips.
I walk to the execution ground, disdainful
of this historic night. In this part of the world
I have no other choice. I will choose the sky

because the sky at least won't decay.
No choice but to die, or else the darkness will be exposed;
I was born in darkness to bring light
and they must kill me to hide their lies.
I object to anything the light won't tolerate, and to silence.
There is a wild gathering of people
deprived of light, darkly packed;
I also stand in this crowd.
I am every person who has died by the ancient methods of torture.
I look sadly
on my own execution,
my blood gushing until I am dry.

5. Unfinished Poem

I am dead.
Bullets left me a body of holes like empty eyesockets.
I have died
not to create a choir of wailing, a tumultuous landscape of emotions,
not so a lone flower will blossom on my grave—
the people are rich enough in feeling.
Each day dew renews the grassland
and rivers drain to the ocean
like ancient wet emotions.
Haven't the people been moved enough?

I am nailed to death on the prison wall;
like a flag rising my clothes slowly drift.

Memorial

I've often thought that
life should have a fulcrum:
Here is that pivot point,
it's this Memorial.

On the Square, at Tiananmen
firm planted on a concrete base
the dignity of the Chinese People is there builded:
Memorial, the fulcrum,
Museum of History, Great Hall of the People,
arranged life the arms of a giant scales.
On one end of the balance is History, yesterday's lessons.
On the other end, Today, our courage, and our future.

The Memorial, darkling quiet, stands there,
like a conqueror, stands there
like a hero who has known defeat a thousand times.
He meditates.

The bones of all the People are his skeleton,
the People's monumental sacrifice, his life.
He is the light that burns from the East's ancient darkness:
all things that must not be forgotten are engraved upon his flesh.
From here
his gaze is fixed upon this world, and Revolution.
And his name shall be called, The People.

I think, and
I am this Memorial.
My body, too, is builded of piled stones.
The weight of the history of the Chinese people
is, just so much, my weight also.
From the countless wounds of the Chinese people
I pour forth just so much, so many drops, of blood.

I stand then
before the Imperial Palace of another morning,
Its gilded culture
my wisdom, and my labor,
my treasures plundered . . .
until the moment the sun rises
and under the purple shadows of glazed tiles . . .
my dream amidst this bitterness.

Here, right here
I have been sold so many times.

Beheaded
my body, bearing still the traces of the chains,
just so, was I buried:
and a living death became the "secret of the East."

Yet all crimes will, in the end, be made known
all debts at last be paid.
When death can no longer be fled,
blood will be bled, and will not clot.
And though the whole earth of the Nation moaned
the sound was the Truth, a high keening, bright and clear.
Because hope burns with an inextinguishable flame,
because the sun always rises,
the truth that curses could not speak
was left to the mouths of the guns.
Revolution gave our blood-anointed banner to the wind
to the sky's freedom.
Well then
it is struggle that's my theme
my poems, my life
I offer up:
Memorial.

Gu Cheng

A Generation

The pitch black night gave me two deep black eyes
with which to search for light.

Discovery

Of all the people who went into the snowy mountains,
Only Bulin discovered the path.
Though there's just a few metres of it,
Though Venus
Broke a tooth there,
None of this prevented
An Englishman from dying,
Lying in the middle of the road, smiling,
Orchids and tender leaves sprouting
From his ears,
And a rosy glow on his face.

What did that mean?
Bulin frowned
And at last he remembered:
When he was nine, he had come
To spend summer, and had planted a box of matches.
They sprouted, and bore
Berries the size of match heads.

The Englishman gobbled them up
Out of greed.

What a discovery!
Unprecendented, perhaps—
    the berry a match bears is poisonous!
Bulin started the trip downhill
And reached the Lama temple made of manure.
He stood stock still, ready to be robbed of his secret
At knifepoint.
But it didn't work out that way. He could only
Sob his heart out
And lash thin copper cables around his stockings
To escape into the deep marshes.

There
Slippers clamoured in a frenzy
And turned into a cluster of frogs.

Who'd Have Thought?

Who'd have thought that
Full stops would turn into peas
Germinating in the night
Drilling through the innards of a hundred masterpieces.

Who'd have thought that
Spain would turn into a mouth organ,
That Lisbon
Would jingle like brass bedsprings
And jangle out a little tune
To let a blind-men's band play for pennies at the seashore?

Who'd have thought that
Bulin would turn bad,
Would carry a toy gun.
He and several Presidents changed their trade
And held up the Bank of France.

Who'd have thought, you've got to think.
That's why you need imagination
To make poetry starve,
To turn it into a dog with a pointed nose, to sniff,
To turn magnified trouser legs
Into savoury tripe.

Bulin Met Bandit

Bulin met Bandit
The one and only Bandit!

Who hails from the river, a scion of
Beast Bighorn, one hand grabbing a beard,
The other grabbing a sword.

He and Bulin
Parried and thrust between
Cracks of brown coal, slicing up
Eight hours and a wrist-watch.

Then Bulin got tired,
He announced: Intermission.
Bandit grabbed
Princess Fibreglass and
Forced her to run away with him.

Oh, what rotten luck!
Who spun fibreglass into a Princess?
It'd make a much better thermos cover.

Runaway?
That's a job calling for
Technique. The most important thing is that
Someone has to chase them—and you must not laugh!

Well, if you mustn't laugh you don't, that's all.

Bandit and Princess
Swam across the pool of the white porcelain wash basin and
Desperately tried to climb the looking glass.
Running for their lives—no laughs!—
But who's chasing them? Where is he?
Bulin said he was tired.
Nothing for it: Intermission.

He and his 15 cents
Are queuing up—for ice cream.

Bulin Is Dead, It Seems

Huge frogs and curses
Were thrown at the wall together.
Bulin, it seems, is
Dead.
Oh woe, at last, God took out a handkerchief to be polite.
A field of square flowers
Broke out
In the graveyard.

Bulin, alas, it seems, is dead.
A hundred yellow-faced grandsons
Came in red limousines from the breast of every continent,
Hurrying here to mourn him. Oh, alas.
They wept for a while, aided by a water pump.
They sawed their teeth, and started dancing
Disco,
Spreading their stubby fingers,
Spreading their mouths, magically producing colourful billiard balls,
Half an ice-cream sun,
A fridge,
And the foam of black beer floating in the sky.

Alas! Alas! Oh woe!
Bulin is dead, dead, dead.

Such well-practised death, as if it were real.
He blinked his eyes in the warm air duct,
Regretted
Not bringing enough
Sleeping pills.

Forever Parted: Graveyard

In Chunqing, at Shapingba Park among weeds and scrub trees, a good way from
the Cemetery of the Revolutionary Martyrs at Geyue Shan, there is a stretch of
graves of Red Guards.

No sign that anyone has been here
but me, and my poems, and what can, what should
I say . . .

1. A Labyrinth of Byways Brought Me Here Among You

A labyrinth of byways
brought me here
among you
like a solitary shaft of sunlight
where the tall grass
and the short trees
rise up together.
I do not represent History
or the sounds
that issue from high places.
I came . . .
because it was time for me to come.

You fell in a heap here
on this ground, together,
tears of joy in your eyes,
grasping imaginary guns.
Your hands were
soft, your nails clean,
the hands of those who'd opened school books
and storybooks, books about heroes.

And maybe just out of habit, a habit
we share, on the last page you wrote
your name, your life, your own story.

Now, on my heart's page
there is no grid to guide my hand,
no character to trace,
only the moisture,
the ink blue dew
that has dripped from
the leaves.
To spread it I
can't use a pen,
I can't use a writing brush,
can only use my life's
gentlest breath
to make a single line of
marks worth puzzling over.

2. The Clouds at Geyue Shan Are Cold

The clouds at Geyue Shan
are cold
like a bloodless hand
pointing toward the graves.
In fire and in molten lead
sunken, silent, mother and father
so
caress the beloved child.
You didn't forget
the words they bequeathed you;
maybe it was just those voices
that called on you to die.
You breathed the same faith
with your very last breath.
You don't really lie so far apart
but on the one side there are still fresh flowers,
lively Sunday visitors
and the Young Pioneers,

and on the other, burrs and beggars' lice,
ants and lizards.

You're all so young,
heads of raven hair,
death's dark night
will keep you so, so pure
forever.

I can wish, I can hope
for the Young Pioneer
for the new fruit
or I can wish I were you,
a wedding picture,
fortunate instant,
that lingers forever,
but I go on living,
mind drawn on, drawn out
like a little boat
bearing slowly
through the dusk
toward the shore.

3. I Don't Have a Brother, But I Believe . . .

I don't have an older brother
but I believe you
are my older brother.
In the sandpile,
in the cicada's shrill,
you made a clay tank
and gave it to me.
You made me a paper plane, too.
You taught me to write
characters, to string them artfully
together.
You were a giant
already in sixth grade.

I have an older sister
but I believe you are also

my older sister,
in the dazzle of morning light
skipping rope,
jumping so high,
turning from side to side
as part of the game
as if the brightly colored strands
could catapult you straight up to the sky,
but they were stretched too tight
and I ended up tangled
from standing too close.

And *him*?
Who is *he*?
who pulled the golden feathers from
the reed finch's wing,
spattering the whole earth
with tiny drops of blood,
or teased the borer beetle
with bounds and flame
and forced him to totter
across a window sill stage
for the crime of eating wood chips?
Who was that?
I don't know him,
a man, only.

4. You Lived Among the Peaks

You lived among the peaks.
You lived behind walls.
Every day you went the way you *should* go,
away from the sea you'd never seen.
You never knew love,
never dreamed of another continent,
another world,
only saw *evils* afloat in a fog;
down the middle of every desk, in chalk
ran the "battle line" of the chess game.
You walked it;
you smiled,

and hid whatever you might be moved to think
if you thought it not right.
Moonlight hidden in the shade of branches:
your law
was unfeeling, pitiless,
and you took that cold sparkle for your festival, your fireworks,
and then, one fine morning
with a handful of dry leaves
you polished bright
the bronze buttons on your leather coat
and departed.

Everybody knew
it was the Sun who led you,
to the tune of a marching song,
off to Paradise.
Later, halfway there
you tired, tripped
over a bed whose frame was inlaid
with stars and bullet holes.
It had seemed to you
a game, a game to play,
a game where you could always start all over.

5. Do Not Interrogate the Sun

Don't question the sun.
Yesterday was not his fault;
yesterday there was another star,
a star that burned away
in the fearsome fire of hope.
Today's shrine holds
carefully selected potted plants
and perfect silence,
the silence of
an iceberg
afloat on a warm current.

When will the raucous bazaar,
when will the patched-up merry-go-round
come to life, start to move again

carrying the dancers or the silent
young, the toothless infants
and the toothless old.
Maybe there are always a few lives
destined to be shed
by the world,
the white crane's feathers
found every day at the camp site.

Tangerine, and pale green,
sweet and bitter
the lights come on.
In the fog-soaked dusk
time heals and we go on living.
Let's go home
and go back to living.
I haven't forgotten;
I'll walk carefully past the graves.
The empty eggshell of the moon
will wait there
for the birds that have left to return.

6. *Yes, I Go Also*

Yes, I am going as well,
to another world, another generation
stepping over your hands.
Though there are fallen leaves
and a scanty snow on the winter sky
I will go on as before.
Beside me—the stones, and the dark grove
and little town as pretty as a cupcake.
I am going to love
and to seek out my soul mates
because it is time for me to go, and to seek.

I believe
that you are the fortunate ones
because the wide earth
cannot flow off
with that arrogant, that innocent grin,

nor will it float up
from the red clay
and be gone.
November's misting rain
when it trickles down to you
will filter out life's doubts.
Eternal dreams
are purer, simpler than life.

I left the cemetery,
left behind the night
and the tangled vines of darkness
still groping
stroking the words engraved on your stones,
groping for you
groping for that life of yours.
Farther off, farther off, the burying ground.
I wish you peace.
I wish the labyrinth of byways
may one day be lost
beneath the new young green of Spring.

Duo Duo

When People Rise from Cheese, Statement #1

Songs, but the bloody revolution goes unnoticed
August is a ruthless bow
The vicious son walks out of the farmhouse
Bringing with him tobacco and a dry throat
The beasts must bear cruel blinders
Corpses encrusted in hair hang
From the swollen drums of their buttocks
Till the sacrifices behind the fence
Become blurry
From far away there comes marching a troop
Of smoking people   1972

There Could Be

There could be days when huge throats gulped down the firewater.
There could be a complete, heroic drunkenness.
There could be one afternoon,
while the clock ticks behind the curtain,
thinking through the heart's trivial business:
there could be persistent, serious embarrassment.

There could be walking alone,
sitting down on a dark green chair

and closing the eyes for a moment.
There could be a comforting sigh
recalling things past that could be called happy,
forgetting the ashes
flicked off, somewhere or other.

There could be, during days of illness,
becoming angry, doing something disgraceful.
There could be following the old habitual pathway,
following the way back home.
There could be someone to kiss you,
cleanse you, and there could also be exquisite lies
waiting for you. There could be a life like this . . .

It could be so good, any time, any place.
A hand, there could be, plucking a fresh flower.
Lips there could be, touching lips.
No more storms, and no more revolutions,
wine offered up by the People to irrigate the soil.
There could be a life like this.
It could be so good, and it will be as good as you want it to be!   1973

Looking Out from Death

Looking out from death you will always see
those whom all your life you ought not to see.
One can always be buried somewhere at one's leisure
sniff around at one's leisure, then bury oneself there
in a place that makes them hate.

They shovel dirt in your face.
You should thank them. And thank them again.
For your eyes will never again see your enemy.
Then from death will come,
when they are consumed by enmity, a scream
although you will never hear again:
Now that is the absolute scream of anguish!   1983

North Sea

Huge shards of glass and ice slash through the North Sea
in such solitude, like the solitude of seas before their creatures found
    the land.
Earth, can you imagine the sky removed?

Tonight wild tigers are boxed up and shipped overseas
and a tiger's shadow slides across my face
—O, I confess to my life

but must confess it is a bore, with not even
the thrill of blood transfusions,
and my memories are weaker than this breeze.

I say that this sea is winding down.
Since I can't trust my ears (where sounds die out)
can't even research laughter's chimes

which can echo from the sea
I say the dimensions of my own body
leave me unimpressed.

Yet beyond the atmosphere are things that make me wild:
eggs laid by stones, or the real world's shadow shifting
in a vertical seabed where currents constantly swirl.

—I've never been happy like this!
I see things for the first time:
this silky river's face, currents arcing like a bridge,

the river shivering like silk as it races through the sky.
Now everything excites me,
a weird joy affects my heart.

As usual, I am rushing around busy,
yet I hear oysters
opening their shells to love

and when lovers weep I detect
a windstorm peeling back the corners of the earth.
The world is silent as if wolves have eaten the last child

and yet, as from a basket high in the air,
I see everyone I have loved
held tightly, tightly, tightly, in one embrace.   1984

Longevity

Feel the heart shiver as bees seek honey, it is that season.
Listen to seeds breathing. Peel back your lids
and see how spots on the backs of milk cows move like the sun's shadow.
The hand of God is a cornucopia spilling over, sun is his fruit.
—the horse lets his eyelids droop,
happy as a fish who has glimpsed the beautiful face of the fisherman.

That's the way things are now. This summer
a train has its leg crushed and the conductor
strides into a field where watermelons
steam in the heat and the ground is strewn with nails of sunlight.
A flock of hens sell their eggs below the sun;
a celestial typewriter marks craters on the moon's page.
The horse takes off a mask made entirely of bone
and the sky brightens. Who knows what it was waiting for?

No more debates. Nothing more to be learned
from ancient breasts, the seven pitchforks,
from sleep and crusted food.
Within the horse's pink brain—a sea pours through the windows
the waves decay, and the anatomies of all things give up,
because they can no longer feel shame.
Sap turns to sugar
as the giant tree sucks shadows out of the soil.
But at the train station the old chess game is still laid out

A seed is rooted deep in memory. The universe
lies in the slender eyes of a fox hunter.
The memory of an orange bleeds through his head
and he hears voices
thickening like cement.   1984

October Skies

October skies drift over the idiotic faces of milking calves.
New pasture, bowing to the May soil, makes its tearful plaint.
A hand snatches up some clay to stop the horse's ears. Listen:
through the dark circles of the underworld,
                      someone is crawling forward
                              on their nails!

Just so, the fingers of my hand become an imaginary plum tree,
my legs become a plough half-kneeling in the clay.
Following the scraping sounds of a steel shovel,
I sweat

to bury the sobbing, deep, deep underground,
and bury the power of hearing beside it:
All that we knew of the sky in our youth,
is laid out under coffin-wood.

The rarified air seduces me:
faces slowly sinking down,
others rising from the old,
conflict becomes an exchange of existences!

Grey clouds roll at the horizon where sunflowers frown:
how many hands withered by lightning, how many heads
                            cutting through the
                            wind.
Sleep now. Open fields. Listen:
the sear grasslands echo with the thin sound of gilded bells . . .   1986

Bell Sound

No bell had sounded to awaken memory
but today I heard
it strike nine times
and wondered how many more times.

I heard it while coming out of the stables.
I walked a mile
and again I heard:
   "At what point in the struggle for better conditions
   will you succeed in increasing your servility?"

Just then, I began to envy the horse left behind in the stables.
Just then, the man riding me struck my face.   1988

Mang Ke

Darling

If your body returns to its first form,
a small heap of yellow earth,
I'm still willing to lie on your full breasts
as I did in the beginning
I'm willing to turn into sunlight
to clothe you in a skin of sun
I'm willing to melt silently with you into one body

If your body turns to spring soil
I'm willing to surrender my own shape
to become water
I'm willing to be sucked up entirely
and with every feeling I have
to saturate your body

To Children

I see you grow lovely, full of the earth
and you open your hands to me like petals
I'm ashamed to show my face
I can give you nothing
I'm neither the sun, your mother
holding you to my breasts, letting you drink my milk,
nor the earth, holding the tray

of day and night in my hand, serving you
scores of beautiful and fine days
I'm just an ordinary man,
but I think of
giving you myself
Grow on my body
Let my heart be sucked empty
by your powerful roots and stems

Vineyard

The vineyard is a tiny patch,
is my succulent home.

When fall wind suddenly bangs the door open
my home is filled with grapes bearing tears.

Startled pigeons lift
from the wall that darkens the courtyard early.

Timid children
hide their dirty faces behind the house.

Dogs usually wander about here;
who knows where they've slinked off to?

A clutter of red chickens endlessly chuckles,
shuddering up and down the courtyard.

Anxiously I watch grapes drop to earth,
bleeding into fallen leaves.

On a day like this I'll find tranquility. I'll never find it.
At this moment my home starts losing sunlight.

Sunflower in the Sun

Do you see
see the sunflower in the sun
Look at it, it hasn't bowed its head:
the sunflower twists its head back
as if in one bite to sever
the rope that the sun
has strung to its neck

Do you see it
see the sunflower raising its head
facing down the sun
Its head eclipsing the sun
The sun is gone
but the sunflower is radiant

Do you see the sunflower
Come up to it and take a look
You will find
its life connected with the soil
and you will immediately feel
the soil spread under its feet
and from each handful of soil you grasp
blood will squeeze out

Poems in October

Crops

Fall comes quietly to my face;
I am ripe.

Labor

I'll drag sun into the wheatfields
with many wagons.

Fruit

Beautiful children,
beauty in their eyes.

Sun like apples in a tree, and below,
a mirage of countless children.

Woods

I don't have your eyes
or your voice.
On the ground a fallen red kerchief.

Wind

I want to tell you
let's go arm in arm.

Path

The white poplar lashes,
a young girl leans against the tree.
Her hopes are lost
on a maze of paths.

Earth

Sun has touched
all my feelings.

Graveyard

Here are no women to knock men off their feet.
Here are no men to make women pregnant.

Dream

Time doesn't care about human nature.
But this brief time together
leaves me breathless.

Poetry

Wonderful, callous imagination
you mould life's wildness.

Sun

You wake again, astonished:
your hair has turned to gray.

Youth

In this land,
in any land of fertility and genesis,
I will be rejected.

Daybreak

If only we were in the same mood
we'd clear the way of darkness.

Testament

No matter what my name is
I want to leave it on this good land.

Yesterday and Today

Yesterday—
it has left nothing
It took away all it should have
But today
what are you like
You're probably shutting the door with great care
You're probably busy catching the lips flying everywhere
Finally they drop to the bed
You're probably waiting eagerly for breasts utterly ripe
to be served on the table in front of you
You're probably stripping someone quickly
like opening a window
but you'll find you can't see the inside clearly
as if it were a darkened empty room
You may have got into the habit of being greedy for sleep
You will probably lie down
but if you lie down
you'll soon dream you've changed so much
you won't even recognize yourself
You always feel
you've been buried someplace
Your body has been rotting,

covered with moss
It looks like you'll be in this daze
all day long
You might have drunk enough liqour now
for blurred parts of a human body to keep reappearing
in your brain
Perhaps you've entered illusion so deeply
you feel your head yanked up
by a mad tree
and swung violently around in the air
or you feel your heart extremely light
like a red balloon
soaring to heaven
You tell yourself it's banished the sun
and taken its place
Maybe now you are parading down the street
tearing off your face
ripping it into confetti
and hurling it about
Maybe, all this is possible,
perfectly possible
Now you stumble into bad times
Now you endure pain
So far you've won nothing
You are at an impasse
or your problem is
you can't make up your mind at all
You have no choice but to have time ridicule you
anyway it likes,
always pulling your beard and moustache
out longer
OK, I want to say my last words
I wonder why I've thought of this
Today is like a barbarian
pinning you to the ground
toying with you as he pleases

Growing Old Even After Death

The white hair of the dead has already grown in the fields.
This makes me believe a person may age even after death.

Even after death a person may still have nightmares pounce on him.
May wake up surprised, open his eyes, and see.

Another day hatches out of its eggshell,
Starts to be busy, pecking around on the ground.

May also hear his own footsteps,
His two legs laughing and grieving.

May also remember, though his head is empty,
Though those in his heart have already rotted away.

May also praise them, may praise his lover,
May with his two hands hold her face steadily,

And then carefully set her in a clump of grass,
Watching her clumsily extract her own sexy body.

May also be waiting, waiting for the sunlight
Which at last the wind whisks away like a scrap of worn sleeping mat,

Waiting for the sunset, which hides from you
As if afraid some beast were about to shred its flesh.

At night this sun passively let you pull it into your arms,
Let you fondle it freely, let you satisfy yourself on it without a word.

May still lie down from exhaustion, close his eyes,
Listening to the roars of hoards of beasts fighting against each other in
    the sky.

May still feel worried, that perhaps overnight
The blood shed in the sky will all flow down on the earth.

May still rise up mourning a dead face,
One with her eyes still staring at you.

May still hope, wishing to live forever,
Wishing not to be an animal, hunted by others

Thrown into the fire to be roasted, devoured,
May still feel pain, may still find things unbearable.

The white hair of the dead has already grown in the fields.
This makes me believe a person may age even after death.

Ape Herd

Prologue

according to legend our ancestors were dust
until one day the drunken princeling sun
stumbled into the boudoir of his sister earth
as if she were his wife fresh from the bath.
their incest so angered god the father
that he made us a gift of his daughter earth
bestowing life on us tiny creatures
granting the choice of form and appearance
flesh and blood and reproductive power,
while the sun received the punishment of fire,
condemned to stoke the boilers for eternity.
through millenia of natural selection
we were born again (they say) so many times
that no one remembers the particular day
when we ruthlessly forsook the ape herd
to become human.
we chose to be human and were proud of our state.
whether in future we will reject it again
and our species mutate into some other form
is impossible to say, and nobody worries.
only when our earth stretches in the grass
like a tawny-pelted cow in *rigor mortis*

and the oven stoker seems hellbent on boiling
us and the carcass into one last stew
do our fears grow wildly and we wonder—
is humanity to be wiped out at last?
do we return to slime? will god let earth rot
and us the maggots teeming on her corpse?
there's no answer. who can guess at god's intent?
our only comfort is to say "its up to him!"

I

a savage beast pounces
with no fear of its savagery
without trembling as it sinks its teeth
do you remember? when was it
that we first learned to use bones,
stripped of flesh, as spears
to grasp in our hands day and night
to protect ourselves
to protect the places we called home
all the women all the children
to protect the love that existed among us?
when did it begin
that we shook our fists at the sun
yelling "watch out!
there's only one of you left
and you're entering my line of fire!"[1]
do you remember? when did
we first realize
we must steal seeds of fire from the sun
set alight the surrounding hostile dark
set ablaze stretches of crazy winter cold
to scare off howling packs of hyenas and wolves?
when did it begin
that we tamed the unchecked rivers
despite their brawling brawny strength
preventing
rape and spoliation
of our fields, as vulnerable as threatened women?
when did it begin
that with throngs of children and grandchildren

we set out to level the mountains
fill up the sea?
when did the longing begin
for our two strong arms
to become wings to bear us aloft
to graze on meadows of snowy cloud
or penetrate the goddess's love garden[2]
(while she's asleep)
and toy with her favourite rabbit!
when began
our fantasy of carefree happiness
diving to the sea floor
throwing our arms round turtles
dancing with dragons
sporting with crustaceans
swimming with the shoal
riding from the Eastern Sea to bob up in the Southern Sea?
do you remember?
when began
the yearning to become as ships
not drifting on life's bitter ocean
but striving for the secret cities of the sea,
archipelagoes, explorations, in quest of joy?
(although in our hearts we understood
that many of us sailing on that voyage
would founder in lonely pools of our own blood)
when did it happen?
when was that?
once upon a time together
we planned to pluck a cluster of stars
those grapes that hang on high
mutually we
understood love and tenderness
became as fire absorbing water
though one might die in the other's embrace . . .
nor should our sword sleep in our hand
our passion should spread to others
like the relay of a glowing brand
no matter how feeble its tips of fire
perhaps already at point of extinction . . .

we also hated
caught and killed birds and beasts
to consume their flesh
and make coats from their feathers and fur . . .
we offered prayers of supplication
for a decent livelihood from the earth we turned
we suffered and grieved
wept tears enough to irrigate our fields . . .
we also knew how to taste pleasure
to rejoice
do you still remember?
how uninhibitedly
we raised the breast-shaped wine pots
body to body in ardent embrace
how contentedly
we drank ourselves blind
we were men as well as women
who might be horses and cattle too
seems like we had no idea at all
what we were
what we are . . .
we could think
we could die
our faces growing like the yellow land
leached and sallow with each passing day
senile and withered with each passing day
gnawed full of rotting wounds
by those gruesome worms of time.

II

it's a good harvest this year
so many corpses are buried in the earth
that the fattened crops have a human taste
and our kids herding on the plain
play and eat as greedily
as calves munching on sweet roots of grass
farm women hard at work
look! their eyes dart
like birds that wing home with food
to hide their gleanings in the dim nest

all the time craning and peering
while those sturdy men
sow their lust in the grainfields
their hands that knead the muddy earth
likewise at certain moments
taking the form
of a randy cock that
all at once springs
on a crouching grass hen.

it's a good harvest this year
see how those new brides
like fresh fish
make their tomcat lovers drool
a man lifts a woman
gently with two hands
as if laying her on a dish
his greedy head bends
like a crow lighting on snow
look again at the dwarf houses alongside
don't worry about the darkness
just poke a hole through the paper windows
and let your eyes slip inside
what can you see?
can you say?
how's the life in there?
or if it's broad daylight
and the sun so stinging
that exposure threatens heart attack
shift yourself into shaded side-streets and lanes
there's nothing to fear from
those street-girls creeping from cracks in the walls
don't be alarmed if
their bloated faces land on your body like toads
don't be scared of
scorpion nests in their bosoms
go ahead and chat with them
what do you hear? you're telling
how life is

it's a good harvest this year
while the night descends like locusts
the sun's rays disappear like wild geese
do you have a home to go to now?
fancy going out to a bar
or a dance hall? yarn a bit
enjoy those grinning buttocks?
what if you get back late
and you've forgotten the key
you think about that person
how will she react?
(since you see he's hours overdue
you're already half asleep
your round breasts and your heart
are hushed, aren't they? or prickling like a hedgehog?
in the middle of the night he staggers in
without a shred of dignity
with the last dregs of blood and sweat drunk dry
would you throw him out?
you wake
eyes open to see that head sharing your pillow
would your lips
those blood-red worms
still desire to crawl over his skin
with their unhurried wriggle?)
after the night is over
and you're still pondering the drudgeries
you've been through in the name of sex
would you discover the shame of your impotence
and the mockery of her two proud legs?
and your brain? would you often feel
your brain to be a wayside pavilion
always deserted
visited by none but transients
with nothing there worth remembering
would you often dream?
what sorts of things would you dream up?
after dreaming you were an ass
would you wake to find the ass has become yourself again

and would you have doubted
whether you became the ass
or the ass became you?[3]

it's a good harvest this year
the dead are still dead
and the living still living
the dead once dead perhaps regret
not dying earlier
while with nothing but their shells
the living drone endlessly
of luck that seldom came their way
of life paid for with pain and toil
mind, are you watching out for your heart?
it may often become like a hungry fish
drawn to the angler's bait
and dragged through the water
by a hook lodged in the mouth

it's a good harvest this year[4]
the sunlight could blacken over
and the flayed skin of daylight
let the days one by one seep to the ground
you could find you are the offspring of monsters
in the lamplight your body
casting the shadow of a runt
a man's head could blow to bits in the crowd
dong dong dong
strikes the bell that is a naked body
two legs could be made to crawl like a tortoise
and humans to learn to see with the eyes of dogs
mouths turning into trumpets
arseholes blaring non-stop talk
    the brightest stars drown in the flood
    while sons of bitches rule the sky
there is love between the stones
while bones are locked in rapt embrace
the faces of the living blow with flies
while rats dare their utmost in the struggle against us
humanity rotten to the core

people nail their own coffins
slander gallops, rumour moves crabwise
carnivores peck their meat,
in the cavities of empty heads
the spider spins at leisure
and one healthy chap
drowns in his own piss
the dead continue their quarrels underground
in heaven the gods are red in tooth and claw
the sun disappears for the distant mountains
like a wounded tiger on the run who stains
his blood across the last of twilight
after disaster
so many are skin and bone
that a gust of wind is enough
to blow them away

it's a good harvest this year
autumn has come around
such a pitiful season!
like a blear-eyed old busker
who stoops
to scratch a coin from the dirt.

III

lonely, unknowing
restless, floating
after disasters without number
from distant isolation
we come.
look, the heavenly bodies scatter before our eyes
like refugees with family and kids in tow
frightened for their lives like we are.
may we ask the cause of the continuing catastrophe?
where did this bloody time come from?
in what direction will the raging torrent
take us tiny beings, infinitesimal as sand?
where will the silt be deposited? where will we end up?

we die again every day and are reborn every minute
our noggins flung across the earth like sown seed

are licked bare by the soil's fangs.
the dead may be contented with sunbeams,
moistened by rain, yet those desiccated skulls!
not a bud has burst, not a shoot, not one
of those skull-seams or eye-sockets has managed
to put forth a waving bough or born fruit aplenty.

our land, dead expanse of land, why does
your body laid waste grow sickly sunshine
bony rocks, jagged stones, that cast hideous
shadows like tombstones, yet warm to each other?
a quite baffling sight that gives an inkling
of how death will be,
a sensation perhaps to be savoured.

for death is after all a matter of choice,
a time when we can discard ourselves
as when the face of the day comes to bury the night.
we can have ourselves thrown into a pit
or burn to ashes while watching our soul erupt
from the physical body and soar into space
to become a directionless voyager
with the best of all vantage points.
already great beast paws trample our torsos,
our heads gradually pull back into the ground.
across the wilderness there echo
the plaintive sounds of our crying
as if bequeathed from remotest history
the tragic gibber of the ape herd.

1. A reference to Hou Yi the archer, a Promethean figure who according to legend shot
down several other suns, leaving only one in the sky.

2. This refers to the moon and Chang E.

3. A parody of philosopher Zhuangzi's Daoist parable: "He does not know whether he is
Zhou who dreams he is a butterfly or a butterfly who dreams he is Zhou."

4. The chaotic language of this section contains references to experiences and rhetoric from
the Cultural Revolution period.

The Post-Misty Poets

Chou Ping

Ways of Looking at a Poet

1

a wreck tossed upon a hazy shore
cursing the delicious banality
of being lost at a familiar place

2

a newspaper wriggled up in wind
and waltzed around on a green lawn
it stumbled over its own shadow
and fell back in a conscious coma

3

a raven in a vacant wood, winging
the black pages of the future

4

a dressmaker's dummy sneaked into a street
looking for King Midas's hand

5

an old man in rags bought a magnolia
to pin it on the flower girl's dress

6

monotonous waves
irresistable countdown of life

7

a sun skated across the ocean
feeling pretty dark inside

8

an admirable punching sack, receiving
every blow with an appreciative bow

9

a rage enclosed in a free balloon
moving up and down in darkness
desperately eager to pierce a hole
and wait for the immediate slow death

10

a broken mirror
with godlike indifference
sleeping open-eyed

11

the slewing arm of a trackless trolley
picking azure flowers from a dark canvas

12

an ant climbs up the sky
in search of a thought

13

a nose practicing saxophone at night

14

a sweet noise
wrapping around one's neck
like a hot towel in summer

Chinese Street

1

A Confucian temple. In the ruinous gateway
two stone lions on pedestals are yawning
as a whirlwind of candy wrappers, Gobi sand, leaves
ascend to the god of order;
coke cans and broken beer bottles
have got together artistically in a mosaic
and wink obscenely at the sun.
They use Morse code.

An old woman in black carries smoking incense in
        her hands
and stutters in a dialect only the Buddha understands.
Here and there on the earth-black roof
a pigeon poses immortally for a snapshot.
Its white wings stand high like a peacock.
Into the 5 a.m. wind a raven
decides to play cards with the zigzag lanes.

        2

Wet stink comes out of the houses like cabbage and
        toilet water
and lazes through purple trumpet flowers
and bamboo fences. The fences have a dusty ambition
to steal gold coins from the sun. Chickens also
drop their stink carelessly
in every court yard.
When the cicada rubs its noisy wings
a baby feels it's time to look for nipples.
Then all the odors settle down in conspiracy
like sneaky dogs. Pure oxygen
is still hanging out somewhere under the moon.
If you walk and leave deep footprints
an obnoxious river of mud, of outdoor sewer water,
of stale rain fills the dents in the earth
with shiny smelly mirrors.

Moments of Love

        I

Hand in hand we float
across a footbridge.
It is a clear night
and your fingers are singing in mine
like a shivering silver tuning fork.
Our steps follow the music
along the sun's orbit.
Suddenly you turn to smile
and your long hair
swirls the stars around.

2

You are gone with the rain,
waving a blue handkerchief.
I am chewing your delicious name
among wild chrysanthemum.

You are gone with the train,
leaving me like an out-of-the-way station
waiting in the evening
for the only passenger to return.

In an Isolation Ward

The sun drops through the room
from a secret passage,
lifting a beam of transparent dust
from the immaculate floor.
I reach out to feel the light—
a sailor holding up fingers to sense wind.

Sunshine moves a pool onto my wall.
A star emerges from behind a pane.
Excited waves beat the stone castle around me—
we roll together back into loneliness.

Life is weightless in a sickbed,
a sea standing up in blue gale.
Is it strong enough to blow the snowcaps
off of mountains and nurses?

O Walt Whitman—"Whispers of Heavenly Death Murmur'd I Hear!"

You are dead, I know,
buried in the rivets of a bridge,

but is that you, or your body, your ashes living in the tombs?
Don't touch me, Walt, I'm a sparrow on a live wire,
it may be death to step from ourselves and connect.
Once I spoke with you, or your shadow in heavy type,
we talked long and forgot who was speaking.
You told me earth may outlive us, or we the earth,
and laughed to tears. I was a bit scared
and the moon offered me a rope ladder through a small window;
my heart was still as an antelope's ears.
It took me a long time to put your words down—
a dust dragon behind a truck is long in settling back to its cave—
and I saw you in streams of dust that stirred with the wind.
You said: don't fall back into yourself
where oranges ripen blandly in the shade
and sunshine is wasted outside like a car running on its back.
You yelled to me again when I saw you at dusk—
you gestured: retreating is a death, dying
        like a hawser coiling on deck,
           a roulette wheel spinning down,
                a circular staircase painted wet,
                a crab nebula burning out;
                you took me in your hand
            like picking up a snail shell
        or the scroll of a broken violin
      and uncoiled me into a river
whorled and fingerprinted with a mysterious force in the dark,
        O Walt Whitman!

Drinking Alone in My Mountain Hut
on a Rainy Night

As the candle flickers in my cup
an inner light snowblinds me—
I feel as dizzy as a window
hanging on a broken hinge.
The rain slips into my hut
through zigzag cracks in the rock wall
or from under the windowsill
until my shoes sail out from under me.

9 Flights Between 2 Continents

Flight 1

In dreams
the continents are apart—
I never mix them up.

1

I take the garbage bag downstairs
and whistle off and on
between awful thoughts and pleasant mail.
It's April again.
It's another crossroad and another continent
and another story of the Monkey King
and the Red Chamber.
Evening despair is gathering force again
on the protruding shadow of ancient tombstones
and slant lamp posts and sleepwalking buses.
Hey, wake up, a voice whispered last night
when I couldn't sleep on my own life.
I gaze into eyes of friends on another continent
and daydream a magic phone, a call
going with night waves across the Pacific.

2

Do you smell a shooting star
or a decaying boat?
Can you touch the dividing line
between day and night on the world map?
Wind keeps rubbing dirt into my eyes.
Suddenly I recall I'm an abacus bead
pushed up and down the eighty-one steps
and I'm grateful
like a still tree with a load of singing fruit
or dying birds.
This is my own darkness,
darker than a dog hidden in a cave
licking its mossy wounds.

3

I know the sun is still outside
but mine drifts apologizing for its dimness

into the age's receding pulse.
Sleeping pills make me loquacious.
Where is the scarlet afterglow
or the pink morning flush on snowy roofs?
Oh, I'm late again about carting hot water
from the boiler on the muddy campus.
Yes. A passport is a certificate
with my own signature on its birth.

4

Look at your smeared face in a steamy bathroom
and there you'll get a wink of reality.
Yesterday, with a forced smile I tamed a ring of wolves
but now I'm frightened
into a salute when a car squeezes to a stop.
I've been trying to tell you my story
but you yawn your teeth out
until our eyes lose each other's whites.
I know my story's taken a wrong turn
and comes out of a zoo with a smelly rhythm.
I know my experience piles up
like essays half-marked and overdue.
I know it's safe to stay at home,
even safer to be thrown in jail.
Look at the guards who protect us day and night
and we don't have to pay them.

5

The plane was so huge—
the moment I stepped in
I lost my shadow.
What is my pulse?
You should have asked me the question
twenty years ago. We all went crazy,
shouting slogans during the day
and practicing lip language at night.
But nothing changed much,
including blood-types.
People still run after the plunging sun
and I joke away my fever
as I wade in slushy dreams.
The old buildings and old books are there.

The past, a sailor
silhouetted against a half moon
on top of a mast at anchor.
Tonight is yours.
Tonight is ours.
We get to know each other,
standing by a bulletin board. A notice says,
GIRLS, CAMP WITH US IN THE MOUNTAINS.
You laugh and I smile.
We linger where the light is.
We float beyond noises and voices.
An icy ectasy tonight when I tell you
how the mud oozes up between my toes
while sun and slogans scorch me in the fields.
My blood runs green against the northern lights.
My skeleton reflects jungle color and vines.
Who said that?
Blood or flood, let it come,
let evil and evil have a duel.
I step over a doorsill and a generation,
carrying half a box of books and folk songs.

6

The ship doesn't answer her helm any more.
We're cut off from the world map's worries.
My atlas is worn at the seams—
sunshine leaks in through the missing cities.
My hut looks shabbier in winter
but I know a friend who will be coming back
when dogs choir in the snow.
I hear your heartbeats clear
like a horse galloping over a stone bridge.
Look, my coat collar puffs up when I walk
and I'll throw the clock back five centuries.
Don't stare at me like an inquisitor.
The tree tops are my fingerprints.
Irregular gushes of wind are my confessions.

7

There was childhood without pocket money.
We stood by the slopes to be picked up by

the carters. I was too skinny to help—
the carters thought—but I was terrific
at my job when the aged masters
chose me. They gave me one or two cents
and a pat on my head. I felt
I should have said, "I'll push the cart up
the slope for nothing." Now days are hidden
like a mountain path through lost forests.
I'm in a landscape painted incessantly
by a wobbling hand. When your eyes open
like a picture book, you care only to pick up
camel bells along the way to an oasis.
You come to feel, not to worship;
but shall we dance to an old record?
I'm bored with disputes, with you or myself.
When a landscape unfolds behind a sliding door,
I recall that rope of sunshine. With it
I can neither climb out of the pit of eternity
nor hang myself. The night is nailed
to a greasy sink by a leaking tap and nightmares.
That holy trinity of night is sticky
like nasty nicknames.
Life is a tedious argument
based on O, O. Oh, no. I'm just
sick and tired of Hiroshima dignity
on this continent. We're all packing
though we don't know where to go.
Dreams of childhood still taste
of peppermint toothpaste, spoiled by
leftovers forced into my stomach.
Am I a stone that no sunny sky could ever warm?
In the flat blue water of my heart, I see
specks of fishing boats and spouting whales.
Don't ask me depressing questions:
We are just process, a way to rot or explode,
we are liquified fury, illiterate fuel
or a snowbank disappearing overnight.
Am I a misplaced book in a library?
Or unmolested hillocks
on the other side of a jammed highway?

8

It was a delayed takeoff from Shanghai.
Nothing can stop me now
after the border guards wave me off.
Not even a heart attack or a plane crash.
I'll smile and sing and shake hands
with death if that's my destiny.
Now I'm a piece of acrophobic cloud. No, I'm
a shivering pane high on a skyscraper,
looking at the illusion of my fall.
I close my eyes and wander down a damp lane,
barefoot on the sunk granite blocks,
floating my dreams into graffiti.
Our house was searched more than three times
and that pain stalks me like a patient's scream.
I'm going. I'm going west through the eastern clouds.
I'm going to look at the world
through the eyes of Taoist ancestors
carting bricks.
This is a dustless land
with occasional skunk nights.

9

Every morning, I bartered at the free market
sauntering between lectures and lettuce.
But here, people find me crazy
when I check out a grocery channel empty-handed.
It will take time to fit in, I know.
Here I'm swinging between continents
when I meet people and talk.
I'm an outsider. That's just fine.
Here, or back home, forever.
When every soul is chatting at a party,
I scrutinize Victorian sketches on the wall
like an extraplanetary idiot.
I walk out,
look around,
see nothing here but Chinese stars.
I should have opened my mouth
but my watch keeps Beijing summer time.

The crowd is thirsty for talk
and togetherness
but I escape—
a habit from the old regime.
My friends live in sumptuous caves,
hang on working phones for dear life.
I'm half a day from jet lag while next door,
in an odd paradise familiar only to my old and new emperors,
America leans cheerfully on one leg.

A Journey to Babel

It's said at the beginning of the universe there was nothing but a chaos of dark-
ness—but who could have borne witness to such lore? It's said that in time im-
memorial the heaven and the earth were not separated—but how could one prove
it with facts? If Darkness and Brightness reign the universe, who can attain an ulti-
mate knowledge of it? If Yin-Yang transmutation started invisibly, who could have
observed and imparted this? So Day and Night thus came out of Ying-Yang—
what is behind such an endless cycle? So Yin-Yang and One formed a Union of
Three—Who is the creator and who is the created? . . .
    —Chuci: "The Heaven Questioned" by Qu Yuan (circa 340–278 BC)

I   The Railroad Station

Voices make the hall a beehive,
people colliding
like thoughts in a crazy mind.
Only the huge clock in the tower
hops around on one leg
hesitantly while trains and desires
ski through stops and delays,
man sailing away in a cage.
The clock strikes one above the faceless mob.

A bird is hovering over the station,
looking for its shadow and fate.
The noises down here must be more attractive
than the murmuring steps through
the Gothic arch and rosary beads.
Saints and hermits are all dead;

who would toast his own shadow
and dance with fantasy today?
Good news drifts down like feathers
from an invisible bird,
yet people argue about its color
until dust soars into the sky
and makes the galaxy a desert.
Random lines are left behind by prophets—
meaningless to those who need,
meaningful to those who need not.
Sudden illumination or sudden illusion
is hiccuped away,
people can only sit on door-sills
to watch ravens in the rain
and see on whose attic they land.

A man moves to the window, asking me
if I have a return ticket to spare.
Yes. I'm on my way
to no place and all places.
In life just leave me alone to travel
on my own feet. My horse has lost
all its teeth and I all my sorrows—
we wander shoulder to shoulder in cities.
I've got a message somewhere in me,
a wind drags at my thin clothes
and at the forests';
is truth revealed only in nudity?
Where is the bird who can
carry this message?
I'm a letter with no address.

I fumble for the ticket.
We all journey—
the sun, a river, disease
through the blood,
old men, babies, salmon,
you and I—
but to where?
Tea is better than beer—

it doesn't pot the belly:
no answer is an answer,
and it helps digestion.
Please leave me alone
to feel the color of the sky
and put herbs on my bleeding feet.
I hand over the ticket;
the man dissolves in faceless noise.

I'm in the shadow of a celestial city,
flying up to you without a cage,
inching forward like a rock climber
on the thread between you and my eyes.
Pull me up to you, my arms are sore.
This is hell—my body, so heavy,
like a mountain, a tide, a cage.
It has roots in the sea of sadness.
O, sharks,
    bite me off,
        let me drop:
the earth is covered with deep snow,
dense forests are a spring mattress
for men with no parachute.
I hate water,
I hate tears,
but I'll keep a salty drop
to prove my identity
in a city of the future.
They would treasure it
like a diamond or a disease.
How is that City?
Mutanies? civil war?
Even worse than down here?
I hesitate
and lose all judgement.

The clock strikes again
and pumps us into a train.
The journey starts
in doubt, in wonder, in a cage.

II On the Way

A coal moon
is pinned
under the only foot
of a lonely tree;
Three shimmering lamps
cross a pool
like a serpent
through waves.
Water.
Hill.
House.
River.
Plain.
I am a wind,
winter wind,
whistling wind.
And I am the locomotive,
the headlight
penetrating
into darkness
along a broken track.
The train is moving
on a square record
and I am the diamond
picking up songs
along the way.

Play the record
the other way round—
we'll spin against
the centripetal death
and come off the stage
with a bang!

A man stands at dawn
watching the train—
an album
folded out
for exhibition.

Destiny windowshopping
for me?

Third-class carriage,
third-class nerves,
third-class sawing coughs,
my fist kisses the table,
a cup throws a somersault.
A man is chewing his teeth
deliciously. He must be
deaf and mute in dream.

A tunnel swallows the train—
fish down a heron's neck.
The gills are filled with soot.
As the air thickens,
sounds thicken,
and the tongue,
and the mind, thickening
until a ball of light flickers ahead.
and we're hauled like deep sea divers
out into a glare of relief.

An abyss of divine light.
An eternal stillness.
Floating with the solar fleet,
I am in the ocean of stars.
Out of junction,
out of orbit,
the train is drawing traceless patterns
in a system of celestial coordinates—
a clove hitch,
a chain of loops,
a lotus flower,
a bird of the soul,
a pair of entangled fish
in a broken net.

III   In Space

Radio waves
squeak in the ionosphere

like blind bats
in neolithic caves.
The air smells:
an electronic shroud
wrapped around souls
who travel here
via endless broadcasts.
Is the rain a result
of the tears of victims?
A tear should be
a monolithic monument—
not a dewdrop
on a blade of grass.
When will the polluted river
clear up again?
When will the world
be free of nuclear sewage?
When will lives
stop bubbling into a bottomless jar
like mountains streams
after a spring shower?
When will poets
stop swirling down like a coat
from the top of a skyscraper,
only churning up indifferent froth?
If one is not afraid to die,
why fear to live?
How can a spoonful of vanity
make a man drunk forever,
making a handful of dust
swell into a colossal idol?
Why is the fossilized war chariot
still dragging a howling black comet behind,
making peace tremble like curtains
in bullet-hole windows?
And why is humanity dying,
a thirsty fish
in South Africa?

The eternal stillness is gone.
I can only vaguely recall

Lao Tzu's bamboo stick
tapping One, Two, Three
from Beyond. Where is
that twelve-doored city?
Is my body only a dream?
What link between DNA
and these thoughts?
Several dark spots
are found on Mars—
are they castles
or skeletons
or ravens
looking for food by instinct?
The setting sun
sits at the shore
of a galaxy,
homesick like a homeless child.
An uncertainty expands
in space
like a wild garden
when the rains come.
Perhaps I shouldn't have
traveled so far
through satellite debris
to encounter the moon
face to face—
you used to be my feather
dropped by a bright-winged bird,
my petal from a budding magnolia,
and I was sad
when a dilapidated wall
cut off half your light,
furious when a slant stake
was wedged into your fullness.
I drifted with you
in swift clouds,
my mood rose
with your silent tides,
but you are now
a solid dream in my hand
—the cooled ruins

of the Tower of Babel.

O stars,
storm-tossed bricks
of the stillborn tower,
exiled poets
from Plato's Eden—
stop yelling
  with your twisting bodies
    in darkness and birthpang,
come down
  in a meteor shower
and build a tower
  in each heart—
Should silence be
  the universal language
    if man recognizes
the inner light
  is
    One?

Xi Chuan

Bats at Twilight

In Goya's drawings they bring an artist
nightmares. They flicker
about him whispering secret things
but never wake him.

Unspeakable pleasures appear on their
human faces. The bodies of these bird-like
creatures are black and wedded to the darkness
like seeds that will never blossom.

They are like fettered spirits,
blind, cruel, led by their wills.
Sometimes they hang upside down on branches
pitiful as dead leaves.

But in other stories, they hang
in dank caves,
and emerge at dusk,
probing for food and giving birth
and then flickering out of existence.

They'll waylay a dreamwalker,
wresting the torch from his hands
and snuffing it dead
or they'll put a prowling wolf to flight
then drop silently through a valley.

If a child can't fall asleep at night
it means a bat
is near, whispering his fate
and eluding the night watchman's tired eyes.

One bat, two bats, three bats,
they are poor and homeless, so how should they bring
us wealth? The changing moon has stripped away their
feathers; they are ugly and anonymous.

Their hard hearts leave me cold,
but one summer at dusk
as I passed my old home I saw the children playing
while bats swarmed above their heads;

twilight spread shadows in the hutong
but the bats were clothed with gold.
They flitted beyond the gate
    with its peeling paint
silent as their own fates.

Among ancient things, a bat
is surely a reminder, and there in the hutong
where I grew up I paused for a long while
watching their leisurely flight.

Southern Horses

Two southern horses dreamed
of a snowstorm shutting the door

Their master slept
like a bear in winter

In the evening the mare
gave birth to a black pony

but the master didn't come
swinging a lantern in his hand

and the three horses
flew across the snow plains

three stars shining
distant

By morning the marks
of their hooves were effaced

In the Mountains

Late sun crystallizes on the steep cliff.
As evening light spills over my tent
sunlight steps away on bouldertops
but it can't escape these mountains.
Past this range the landscape opens.
My four horses are lost in the plain.

This book winds down to a final word.
I am alone at dawn
outside the tent
feeling sand pummel the whorled water.
My horses dispersed in four directions
shed tears in the wind.

In their scarlet hearts
firetrees and silver flowers are sudden constellations.

Night Birds

Night's remnant almost gone
and birds (of what color)
slip over the city.

They could be just there or far off,
that happy tribe, their cries
like thoughts in a dream.

Birds (of what color)
soar off with secrets
and forgetfullness.

The calls of summer leaves
or a stream in autumn
can't compare with theirs,

though I see not a single
body. Maybe they are
just some happy sounds.

Seven Nights

—For Bert Stern

I.

As night alights gently as a bird
a drop of rain falls on my brow.
On the Telegraph Building rooftop another one drops.
In the darkness of the east
I see the winds of Asia pensively
stirring in the leaves of the trees.

2.

The water slipping through the wasteland
is silent and clear; far off,
my blue pony still lacks form.
Beyond the city all is desolation.
A rider solemnly
presents me with a city and a dream.

3.

In the silence at midnight
I often cross this city of shadows,
shadows, thieves among the ruins,
shadows, lovers in doorways,
shadows, young people dancing into the night
unable to stop.

4.

The bell of loneliness tolls without being struck.
Melancholy is second nature to a homesick man.
But it's even stranger living here
homesick at home
as if you'd wandered for years
and suddenly remembered a familiar moonlit path.

5.

Oh Michaelangelo, so far from you,
weary man, interpreter of nature.
You dream of a nightingale and her garden.
You dream of a woman, naked on a sarcophagus.
Only in your work do you find comfort
yet still you doze in this cool breeze.

6.

In my penniless country
I calmly await an uninvited guest.
Perhaps his hair is white.
Perhaps his stride is proud and confident. I know
my last dawn will dawn forever.
I open my door and listen into the night.

7.

A drizzle the temperature of Heaven's lonely court
where we will drift tonight—
another city of brilliant lights.
The stones of my back courtyard are cool.
Someone who praises the night is dropping through sleep.
In another city someone else is waking up.

The Book of the Past

When the ship of dawn anchors
        the ship of evening sets sail
and Venus shines, guiding souls
over vineyards and stables which offer
        in a passing instant

gifts of fruit and ripeness
to those light-fearing faces.

The figs of dream tremble on a plate.
Pictographic cypresses and pine trees construct
        a city on the peak.
So much useless perfection, as Venus
sinks and moonlight pours over
a barren path in the north.

O, ancient moonlight, silent earth!
Walking through the dark gate I hear the long-winded wind,
I see naked petals
illumined by a sacred fire
and have faith in the future's immanent body.

Only this poem will vanish
and the nature of time will come clear,
incessant time—though what is past seems near,
like the moment after a storm,
when the storm's mother still perches in the treetops.

Venus pardons both good and evil
and this the souls know, familiar with
        the barren path
and the world's sad shadows.
Rising for what is departed, the sun pierces
like a woman's shrill cry.

 # Zhang Zhen

A Desire

He is the color of September
and graceful like autumn weeds that wilt
each day below my bicycle's lonely wheels
and wave to me from all sides
like young girls' wine-blushed arms
Signs of his brightness, his innocence
but for me this shock of color
radiates only violence
He begins by kissing my neck
then smears burning liquor all over my body
His hair stands up like noon sunlight
I am begging
but he climbs over the mountains where my soul lives
and then drifts away
Only the double oars we have used are left
in the reeds corroding

Abortion

The sky keeps flashing
Beyond it
you beautifully take form
humble, a helpless bird
You are my little bird

on the verge of a fatal slip
There is no umbilical
and I despair

For this imagined relationship
mother and son
you and me
I've already sharpened the knife
Blood fireworks up in glorious patterns onto the ceiling
A pair of skinny legs upside down

That was my love
You should have been a golden glory like an ancient urn
But it is hard to say, you might have been a stretch of dead black
covering this window of mine. O god
such relief! I'll drink toasts till I'm sick drunk.

That was also my hate
I looked long into my uterus at your unwarranted being
I labored over those hills in a neck-on-neck race against you
In the end only I was saved

Now if I want to call you back what language should I use?
You hang on my knees listening. But I have no fables to tell
Your mother has only many secrets. You are one of them

Now walking in front of the funeral band
in full bright red I hold up a torch-bouquet of poppies
Your brothers and sisters will all be informed
that you are the oldest son, prior to all
the most beautiful
I am forever proud of you

Everything is normal at home
pacing between window curtains
I miss the you I never see
Candle flame brings out your special smell
I never give birth to you
But whenever I dress up to go out
I see you and me in the same mirror   3/26/86

New Discovery

An accidental discovery
between the bedroom and living room
It is a fate between these doors
attracting me with its magnetic field

But the tremendous window
reveals a generous night scene in front of me
—houses sleep with houses
The city pushes me on

Night is a long corridor to heaven
I rush along barefoot
A huge arrow hits me as if it were my fate
and sends me into this open darkness

The discovery is our body
female essence
Night turns her into an angel
and the room fills with dark blue star-clusters

Magnetic field of the navel
A lunar halo slowly expands
I drive a wheel-less horsewagon through
a colored field stretching into this deep valley   3/24/86

The New

In an old photo a clock's finger
is nailed to a silent coordinate.
Steel rust winds about the house.
He enters and then collapses
and layers of dust fall like snowflakes.
An inspiration, not mine, shoots from the closet.
Perhaps my wings lift
an imaginary feather—
this can never be verified.

Exhausted seeds send signals from every corner:
who are you? Who are you?
My flower outshines all flowers,
my tears drown other tears,
but still everything remains:
some sediment,
an ocean waiting to boil,
a blurred demon shadow.
Each night makes me sink deeper.

Homeland

Listen: a crass celebration outside.
Wind in the trees drowns all human sound;
voices rise again like Atlantic tides.

I recall the ocean liner to this place:
summer, like today,
but vision was walled in by fog.

This will be a sleepless night.
The doorbell blares: urgent telegram,
a major rainstorm is confirmed.

Norway—the name is special today.
"Out of mist, she appears—"
my husband is half-drunk, singing the anthem out loud,
only half of him from this country,
but he's like a new man.

This happiness saturates everything
but I sit alone before a glowing copper mirror:
in the distance a face.
The sea simply collapses
and my small boat is nowhere.

These dusty images
are especially vivid
as I meditate on the night wind.

The celebration climaxes.
I've never seen Sweden's famous glaciers.
They must be melting.

The footprints of my pilgrimage cross
a swampland where spirits live,
my heart freshly marked by deer hooves,
strawberry juice spilling from my hair.
After making love here
I know this word, "homeland."

Deep into Smaland

On a trip
I close my mind's eye.
The weather bounces around
and messes up my timetable.
Then in the middle of this lake,
a stretch of water about to be eaten by mud,
the real colors start to appear.

Under my feet
the reeking graves of the past generation
torture me.
Not Tiananmen
nor Golden Gate Bridge
but coming back here is to arrive at a conclusion.
It's baffling as the perpetual rain.
No one else can know this.

I won't swim here;
the Asian-blood-happy mosquitoes would chew me up.
And through the clusters of lotus blossoms
water snakes thread,
their skin as beautiful as black jade.
Our eyes meet across the silence.

This sight
slowly sinks in me.

Now the darkness of this cypress and pine province
covers me with layers of silk,
fresh moss still spreading sweetness of the past,
wet and heavy.

The nature of this place
is a bad fit with my past,
yet sometimes I glimpse
my life's other half.

Sometimes I can think back that far:
the aged thorn trees and stone steps
force me to consider:
should I be buried in this foreign land
or drift back like white rain
and drop into the lake of my hometown?

—as if that place would ever let me return.

# Tang Yaping

Black Night (Prelude)

I can't stop this darkness leaking from my eyes
When the night seeps out I am vagrant
a night-walking goddess in total black
Light-wheels in the mist spin through the night like bees
These obscure colors saturate me with dark knowledge:
all colors harmonize on the way to black
Wandering goddess, the best child of pain
these fat-pawed cat feet and snake body
evade the cockcrow with stealthy humor
In this deep night what am I doing
becoming a shadow with a real body
or playing half in dream, in the shadow of all things?
"She is truly the best, the best the best"
A night wind stirs in my black gauze kerchief
I feel graceful, so easy, I am floating
At night everything is the shadow of a mirage:
skin   blood   flesh   bones   all blacken
baffling   baffling   baffling
Even the shadows of sky and ocean are night

Black Nightgown

I fill a bottomless bottle with water and bathe my feet
Nights when it rains are most interesting
I've asked a man over to talk
Before he comes I do not think
—I pull down the purple sash and turn a pink wall-lamp on
My black nightgown does three rounds about the room
—then the door is knocked on three times
He comes in with a black umbrella
and opens it up on the floor in the middle of the room
We start to drink strong tea
Noble compliments pour like piped water
Sweet lies shine like bright stars
Gradually I lean back on the sofa
and with scholarly passion tell the story of an old maid
The god that was between us runs away
covering his ears and without one slipper
This evening of talk leaves me dizzy
When telling a story
the darker the night the better it is
and the heavier it rains the better

Black Swamp

Evening is a blurred moment
a dark instant that would make a dog nervous
I jump at my own shadow, can't even sit or stand still
as my hair strays wildly with desire
        and I am ravished by night
This desire an endless darkness
I keep stroking the darkest spot for a long time
watching as it turns to a black vortex
powerful enough to seduce the sun and moon
Horrible—I can't escape this darkness
which strips me bare and leaves me panicky
Yet in this death I find the courage
to give in completely, taking in everything
going even deeper into the black swamp

I'm a born cynic, I was born a dupe
Before my birth my mother foresaw some convulsion
Tonight nightmare will break the thin ice
and make memory sink and drown
All that I want to drown is sucked under
only a beam of ancient sunlight remains unsubjugated
My silence sticks in the dark throat of night

Black Tears

Who told that child to play ball on the square
and make my heart leap up and down,
resounding like a slow drum?
Sometimes we all need to roll in the dirt
I never knew God made so many people
or all these bodies created just one god
but every life rules me like a god
Whose lazy footsteps keep coming around?
For a thousand minutes I gaze
        at the chipped edge of a china bowl
A thousand minutes together make a night
Black loneliness drips black tears
Tilted dusk collapses on me
I plug my hands into the night
and hold on as if I could fall at any moment
Why am I nervous about losing my life
when I have other things on my mind
        I need to get rid of first?

Black Gold

Already I wither
already am docile and obedient
Common men are tortured by my pride
My talents frustrate potent men
My eyes are chasms
Misfortune infects my blood

and my milk turns into tears of acid
The problem with me is the problem with gold
—everyone plunders me
        then hoards me with all the love there is
Each night is a chasm
All of you possess me
        only the way night holds fireflies
Listen. My soul will turn into misty smoke
to make my corpse docile and obedient

Black Cave

The black cave's darkness shrouds day and night
Bats dive in clusters through the arching cave
Wings whip up gruesome and obscene charm
In a glorious moment women disappear in a blind world
Whose hand points to the skyless exit?
A hand of bones reaches out
and kneads female roundness to edges and corners,
palm up and clouds tremble, palm down brings rain
It drags a woman out
makes her have eyes and lips
makes her have caves
Whose hand is that? reaching out
to expand the sky of no exit
It is a hand of bones sticking out
to gather the sunlight on its fingers
It burns fingerprints on her breasts,
pours stalactites into her cave
Palm right you touch heaven, palm left you're back on earth

Black Midnight

I light up a cigarette and walk through the dark
The night roams in the footsteps
        of a woman's animal heat

Desire remains bloody red
and flashes in its endless search
Empty smoke-doughnuts float in the sky
Stars pale to a cruel, impassionate stare
A gigantic black shadow covers a seven story building,
a black moan coming from every window
And now only one wish remains—
to murder, torch the place, break into someone's home
A decrepit old bachelor
rips a woman's shirt sleeve from her arm
seizes her near-extinguished cigarette butt
then mercilessly drifts into the night

Black Rock

Looking for a man to torture her
a beauty with tiger teeth smiling
lives in the footprints of suicide
She's tough but she finds only despair
The empty earth, the blank sky,
are deep as you want them to be
This dead rock was also rock when alive,
had nothing to hate, nothing to love,
nothing to be loyal to, nothing to defect from
The more the sorrow, the more the joy
Let some inconceivable idea control everything
A hairy little bird has pecked away all stupid responsibility
A head refuses to let a dream enter
Circulating blood spills disaster everywhere
Now the forbidden fruit is full and ripe;
it will be seized without foreplay
Pregnant womens' faces are everywhere
Freckles seem to butterfly off
The nightmare mystifies, but it thrills
You've got to convulse while alive

Fei Ye

The Curse

The moment I wake up I'm inside a dream:
The bed is surrounded by hit men,
Teeth snatch at me from the mirror,
Each day and night is a season in hell,
My open eyes nail through the wall
To a vision of earth carpeted with sickbeds.
In a newborn face you can see the century's absurdity—
Hit men and victims depend on each other
And there is no road to the past, never has been.

The instant I get up I start to remember,
Boat adrift in the mind's river,
Where does this clean water go?
You won't even catch your reflection in it.
At daybreak the end is clear.
Silence, the greatest weapon, has been brought to bear:
No words, no songs, no crying.
Quick as flicking the light off at bedtime
Let earth return to primordial calm
As stars pursue their ancient games
And the people wait for death and gape like fish.

The Poet in America

O poet, why do you suffer?
O singer, why does your voice break?

America, I can't see you.
I will never get out of your ghettos;
I can't see your face past those skyscrapers.
America, did you know
That Kafka is right above Fei Ye's head
Looking over today's Castle?
He gives me hope for progress,
And makes young punks my brothers and sisters.

Life in America is like science fiction,
America where cars like armored beetles crawl,
Airplanes hover like flickering dragonflies,
And the people's faces droop like dogs.

Whitman, you old schemer,
The TV antennas have snipped your great beard.
Your sons and grandsons
Have only the pain of poverty.
Murder, suicide, nothing is new in America
        of which you sang.
O poet, quickly, help me aim this missile—
Should I, a final time, check out the prices
        in this human meat market?

We Are Little Creatures on a Little Planet

We are little creatures on a little planet.
Beyond the day sleep awaits us.
Since the sun leaves us with no farewell,
Dinner turns sour in the stomach,
Light in the room is dim and strained,
The shadows seem to fill with geese and goats.
We are tiny creatures, our senses numb,

We can't see how the eastern sky kindles,
We just huddle in one corner of the bed,
Our fear shot through with dreams
Of childhood friends we won't meet again.
Dark thunderclouds grumble distantly,
Random message sent to a small planet
By a god living on a far off star.
Below this tent of dead-black clouds
We tremble and shake.

Singer in a Red Century

In a wink
Gold semen spills all over the earth,
Flowers blow, fruit ripens, and humanity persists:
The cruel crimson emperor issues decrees,
Mozart echoes through the house all day,
And you who sing at the dusk,
Your hoarse, tired voice calls out endlessly,
Louder, louder and more hoarse.

In the empty room you stand punchdrunk;
There is nothing to do but sing.
Wild strawberries recite in silent rapture
And released from the forms of loyalty
        the tongue is set free at last,
Yet the saved tongue says nothing at all.
Get going, hit the streets, though you die there—
Singer in a red century, witness of atrocity,
Your silence will explode in the dead of night
And the world will never again know peace.

Ceremonial Praise

The sun at the bottom of a green beer bottle
has found its home

Aimless flowing blood
makes fingers and leaves tremble together

The person in a dream of morning
left before the liquid flash

The birdman of four beaming eyes
no longer sings with grief

A large golden clock
hangs forever in your heart

Bei Ling

Impression

clouds flocks of bird flying nowhere to perch
plumage crowds the sky   sifting down
felt hat   black felt hat   lost
confluence of oilcloth umbrellas   wooden bridge cracking
     I am running in circles

Notes in Winter

Amazing how far amazing how dim
Everything is held up behind time
Those wild days filled with triumphantly scribbled
     ornamental words
days with folded arms
remote . . . you try to reach back but your hands are blocked

Winter chaos
Winter can't retain the sunlight
You are far from everything
but your feet still rush

Nothing, nothing left
no naked trail twisting into two
no wind blowing across the roof
no words found through suffering

When aroused, strange sounds will float up
Human sound
The sound of light and excrement

Serenity of the whole night

Notes in Autumn

Here lie some words of the past
Words in front of me
Heartbeat   of a heavy oiled
drum   While veined autumn
inches forward
stormy waves of underwater silence

Year after year   remember
all that unstable night   horrible
night of autumn   night of brave calm
Though wind is a swallowing whirlpool
surging up endlessly
the door is left open

That was when the shriek shot through the wall
and whirled into a trembling song
You walked in tedium
jumped on a train
You walked through the jammed streets
and faded in the rushing mob

Autumn is not a deep valley   it has no empty rooms
but stands rigid in the atmosphere
These word characters are no cold companions   not

cruel characters   indifferent characters
behind gold circles and spots of time
They will make another inquiry

I Don't Need This

I don't need this: to be bitten
again, by spring, by time's defiled love
As logic is lost
dreams swell with impulses
As thought is drained again of blood
it pales and is caustic
evidence of the heart suffering
I don't need this

Here I am, looking like a folding screen
and here's a figure, finger to the pulse
Here's the sunshine all bottled up,
plentiful, void
and reasonable

deep inside.

Ha Jin

Our Words

Although you were the strongest boy in our neighborhood
you could beat none of us. Whenever
we fought with you we would shout:
"Your father was a landlord.
You are a bastard of a blackhearted landlord."
Or we would mimic your father's voice
when he was publicly denounced:
"My name is Li Wanbao. I was a landlord;
before liberation I exploited my hired hands
and the poor peasants. I am guilty
and my guilt deserves ten thousand deaths."
Then you would withdraw your hard fists
and flee home cursing and weeping like a wild cat.

You fought only with your hands,
but we fought with both our hands and our words.
We fought and fought and fought
until we overgrew you and overgrew ourselves,
until you and we were sent to the same village
working together in the fields
sharing tobacco and sorghum spirits at night
and cursing the brigade leader behind his back
when he said: "You, petty bourgeoisie,
must take your 're-education' seriously!"

Until none of us had words.

The Execution of a Counter-Revolutionary

It is no use to beg anymore.
He has begged them many times
to let him speak to the head of the army hospital,
but he's told nobody will listen to him,
a bad egg, who only deserves a bullet.

"We've been ordered to get your skin,"
the squad leader says, "to repair
the extensive burns of Liu Yi
who risked his own life
saving horses from the burning stable.
Now, let's go."

They take him to the hill behind the hospital.

It's dinner time
and the loudspeaker is playing music.
Nobody will hear the shot in the woods.

They stop at a ruined temple
whose stones, bricks and rafters
have been ripped off by the villagers.
In the distance
a light is shining like a glow worm.
He doesn't know whether it's a star or a lamp.
It doesn't matter now.
He takes it as the pole star.
His only worry is: I'm not nineteen yet
and my parents will never know
how their son disappeared.

"Now you may say something if you want."
They pull the towel out of his mouth and wait.

Suddenly he starts yelling, "I curse all of you,
the whole hospital! All your babies
will have no assholes and die at birth!

I curse Liu Yi and his family too!
He and his folks will be struck by thunderbolts!"
They raise their pistols
and he raises his tied hands:
"Long live the Chinese Communist Party!
Long live—"
One pistol fires.

He wanted to shout "Chairman Mao,"
but they wouldn't let him get it out.

The bullet hit his penis—
which is the best way to save the skin.

An Old Red Guard's Reply

Having been wrecked so many times
we will not set sail once more.
Having been deceived again and again
nobody could care whether there is any truth.
Try to persuade us,
portraying the magnificent deeds of the old days
or promising us a golden monument in the archives.

Our old hearts, burnt out by dreams, fell
like meteors on the shore
and transformed into these rocks
that cannot be shaken by the great waves.
Our legs were amputated on the tables
which we once mistook for stages
where we enacted the Dance of Loyalty.

Now we cannot move,
either toward the sea or toward the land.
Whatever you say, our tongues,
which finally have learned how to voyage,
will reply, "Yes sir."

They Come

Sometimes when you're walking in the street,
returning home or leaving to see a friend,
they come. They emerge from behind pillars and trees,
approaching you like a pack of hounds besieging a deer.
You know there's no use to hide or flee,
so you stop and light a cigarette, waiting for them.

Sometimes when you're eating in a restaurant,
your soup served and your dish not ready yet,
they come. A steady hand falls upon your shoulder.
You are familiar with such a hand
and don't need to turn around to meet the face.
The scared diners are sneaking out,
the waitress's chin is trembling when she speaks,
but you sit there, waiting patiently for the bill.
After settling it, you'll walk out with them.

Sometimes when you open your office,
planning to finish an article in three hours,
or read a review, but first make some tea,
they come. They spring out from behind the door,
like ghosts welcoming a child to their lair.
You don't want to enter, seeing cups and paper on the floor.
You're figuring how to send a message home.

Sometimes when you have worked day and night,
dog tired, desiring to have a good sleep
after taking a shower and an extra nightcap,
they come. They change the color of your dream:
you moan for the wounds on your body,
you weep for the fates of others,
only now dare you fight back with your hands.
But a "bang" or an "ouch"
brings you back to silence and sleeplessness again.

See, they come.

An Escape

We sat in the neon lights
on a cool evening of a summer day
drinking beer and eating salad.
You told me your story
similar to those of many others:
All your savings are gone,
the managers, the secretaries, the supervisors,
the police in charge of passports,
all received a handsome share;
now you have nothing left there,
your color TV and refrigerator were sold
to get the cash for the plane ticket.

"But I was lucky," you assured me.
"Many people have spent fortunes
and still cannot leave that country."

"What are you going to do here?
Don't think this is a country where
you can make a fortune by snapping fingers.
Starting poor, we have to labor for every dollar.
It is a place where money
can hire the devil to make bean-curd
and one's growth is measured by financial figures.
There is no way for us to get beyond
a social security number."

"Anything, I would do anything,
as long as I can make a living.
At least, I am free here and don't
hate others. Do you know what I wanted
when I was back there?
I always imagined how to get a gun
so that I could shoot all the bastards.
That country is not a place to live—
I would die rather than go back."

We stopped to watch sea gulls.
An airplane was writing the word
FUN in the distant sky.
I wish I had left in the same way.
I have brought with me all my belongings,
even my army mug and a bunch of old letters.

A General's Comments on a Politician

He is no politician
because he has rubber hands
and doesn't know it is necessary to kill.
He watched his enemies developing in eggs,
and observed how they broke the eggs
and became nestlings.
He thought they were chickens,
but one day they flew to the sky
and changed into hawks.
He doesn't have the guts to crush the eggs!

When I was a battalion commander,
our neighbor battalions always suffered
from the enemy's artillery.
They knew there were some agents in their units
who informed the enemy of their movements,
but they couldn't find them out.
This never happened to my battalion,
because I did not bother to find them out.
I just shot the few persons I suspected.
As the head of a whole battalion
I could not put four hundred lives at stake.
To be sure, I did it secretly. At night
I brought them to a grove one by one.

A politician must have iron hands,
although you may wear gloves over them;
just as a general must never worry about
how many wronged ghosts cry
after he puts his sword into its sheath.

Marching Toward Martyrdom

The commander gave orders
and we started marching.
We swung our hands vigorously up to our second buttons,
and watched each other through the corners of our eyes
to keep our bodies in a straight line.
We marched as if we were on parade,
although we knew these were exercises.

But we stopped before a deep trash pit,
and kept marching in place on its edge.

"Go ahead! Who told you to stop?
If you kill yourselves
your families will know you are martyrs!"

We marched on.

It was so easy to become a martyr,
and there were so many ways.

Because I Will Be Silenced

Once I have the freedom to speak
my tongue will lose its power.
Since my poems strive to break the walls
that cut off people's voices,
they become drills and hammers.

But I will be silenced.
The starred tie around my neck
at any moment can tighten into a cobra.

How can I speak about coffee and flowers?

UNIVERSITY PRESS OF NEW ENGLAND publishes books under its own im-
print and is the publisher for Brandeis University Press, Brown University Press, University
of Connecticut, Dartmouth College, Middlebury College Press, University of New Hamp-
shire, University of Rhode Island, Tufts University, University of Vermont, and Wesleyan
University Press.

ABOUT THE EDITOR

Tony Barnstone's critical edition of the poems of the Tang Dynasty poet Wang Wei (*Laugh-
ing Lost in the Mountains: Selected Poems of Wang Wei*, co-translated with Willis Barnstone
and Xu Haixin) appeared in 1991 from the University Press of New England. He has pub-
lished poetry, book reviews, essays, and translations from Spanish and Chinese, as well as his
original artwork, in a number of American journals, including *American Poetry Review*, *The
Literary Review*, the *Centennial Review*, the *Berkeley Poetry Review*, and *City Lights Review*. He
will be the Asia editor for an anthology of the literature of Asia, Africa, and Latin America,
forthcoming from Macmillan. His current project is a book on William Carlos Williams and
materialism.

Library of Congress Cataloging-in-Publication Data

Out of the howling storm : the new Chinese poetry : poems by Bei Dao . . . [et al.] / edited
by Tony Barnstone.
   p.   cm. — (Wesleyan poetry)
Includes bibliographical references.
ISBN 0-8195-2207-4. — ISBN 0-8195-1210-9 (pbk.)
   1. Chinese poetry—20th century—History and criticism. I. Pei-tao, 1949–
II. Barnstone, Tony. III. Series.
PL2333.O95 1993
895.1′15209—dc20   92-56899

∞